John Mactta
July 2001

JEFFERSON'S WEST

A Journey with
LEWIS AND CLARK

JEFFERSON'S WEST

A Journey with
LEWIS AND CLARK

James P. Ronda

Preface by Robert M. Utley

THOMAS JEFFERSON FOUNDATION

Monticello Monograph Series

2000

Cover inset photographs: portraits of Meriwether Lewis (left) and William Clark (right) by Charles Willson Peale, courtesy Independence National Historical Park. Background art includes portrait of Jefferson taken from 1805 portrait by Rembrandt Peale, courtesy New-York Historical Society (accession number 1867.306), as well as details from Clark's journal and field notes (courtesy of the Beinecke Rare Book and Manuscript Library, Yale University, and the Missouri Historical Society).

This book was made possible by support from the Martin S. and Luella Davis Publications Endowment.

*Thomas Jefferson, by Rembrandt Peale, 1805
(New-York Historical Society, accession number 1867.306).*

PREFACE

IN 1803 THOMAS JEFFERSON bought Louisiana from France. It was arguably the most consequential act of his presidency and certainly the one that most glaringly violated his constitutional scruples. He had intended only to ensure that no foreign power ever used New Orleans to plug the commercial waterway of the Mississippi River. But, suddenly offered all Louisiana—whatever that might be— he seized the opportunity.

In Thomas Jefferson's mind, the Louisiana Purchase brought together both national interest and personal interest. His vision of the young republic's destiny was continental in scope. So was his intense geographical curiosity. In the service of both his nation and his mind, he had already commissioned Lewis and Clark to explore the western reaches of the continent. It was then foreign soil. Now, in some uncertain part, it was American.

Thomas Jefferson and his two captains still resonate in the public imagination. Less evident to modern generations is the chasm separating the West that Jefferson pictured from his Virginia mountaintop from the West that Lewis and Clark confronted in their transcontinental trek.

As one of his major themes, James Ronda explores this chasm and its implications. He contrasts the optimistic view from Monticello with the hard reality of the upper Missouri and the Bitterroot Range. He traces the origins of Jefferson's conception and shows how it shaped the purposes and results of the Lewis and Clark Expedition.

Jefferson's image of the West reflected the consensus of the scientific community. Beyond the Missouri River, the fertile, well-watered lands of lower Louisiana extended to the Rocky Mountains, an inviting "garden" for the yeoman farmer so dear to the president's heart. The mountains themselves lifted no higher than his own Blue Ridge and presented no serious obstacle to transcontinental passage. The Missouri headed there, navigable all the way to the Mississippi. A short portage from the sources of the Missouri, the "river of the West" offered a navigable descent to the Pacific.

As Ronda makes clear, this geographical perception underlay the primary objective of the Lewis and Clark expedition: to find an easy way across the continent for American commerce to flow to the Pacific and on to the Orient. Here again was the time-worn quest for the elusive "northwest passage."

Jefferson specified other missions as well: map and describe the route; record for scientific scrutiny every detail of geography, climate, plant and animal life, and human inhabitants; bring back as many representative specimens as possible. And finally, clear in motive though unmentioned in orders, beat the British across the continent. He had read Alexander Mackenzie's *Voyages from Montreal,* in which the veteran fur trader called for British colonization of the Pacific Slope. That, Jefferson fervently believed, should be accomplished by Americans.

By contrasting the wilderness struggles of the two captains with the felicitous landscapes of Jefferson's mind, Ronda dramatizes the breadth of the chasm between geographical theory and geographical reality. He also incidentally reveals why the expedition, whatever its other results, failed to achieve its central objective. In short, there simply was no northwest passage.

What Lewis and Clark discovered instead was a continent much wider than anyone conceived. The northern Rockies were no benign Blue Ridge but range on range of towering heights daunting in magnitude and complexity. The headwaters of the Missouri barred navigation even by canoe. And the easy portage to navigable waters beyond turned out to be several hundred miles of the most rugged mountains in North America. Nor did the Great Plains east of the Rockies resemble the beckoning agricultural fields of lower Louisiana.

Another of Ronda's major themes also exposes a chasm between rival understandings. Lewis and Clark entered an Indian world that neither they nor their patron could comprehend. Even direct experience failed to strip the captains of stereotypical preconceptions. Most of the tribes proved friendly and helpful. The explorers never perceived their hosts as motivated in large part by the promise of trade goods, especially arms and ammunition with which to contend with enemy tribes. Patronizing lectures about their new Great Father and his demand that they live in peace with one another and with the white newcomers fell on bemused if not puzzled ears. They had their own world view, and the awkwardly translated words changed no traditional patterns of intertribal warfare. Indeed, the only armed collision with Indians occurred when a party of Blackfeet understood what the standard message meant: their enemies, hitherto disadvantaged by British rifles in Blackfeet hands, were about to be equipped with American rifles.

As Ronda perceptively notes, Thomas Jefferson and the Corps of Discovery explored two Wests at the same time. Lewis and Clark explored "visible landscapes;" Jefferson explored "the country of the imagination." And so the world of Thomas Jefferson hardly overlapped the world of Lewis and Clark, and the world of neither shared any commonality with the Indian world. Yet in one sense all three are connected: they form a significant chapter in the early history of the United States, the first of a series that culminated in a nation of continental dimensions.

As a compelling part of the American heritage, this story deserves telling and retelling. James Ronda is uniquely qualified to tell it. He has explored all three worlds and written with insight and authority about all three. Equally important, he understands how all three interacted—or failed to interact. His is a story for all Americans.

— ROBERT M. UTLEY
April 21, 2000

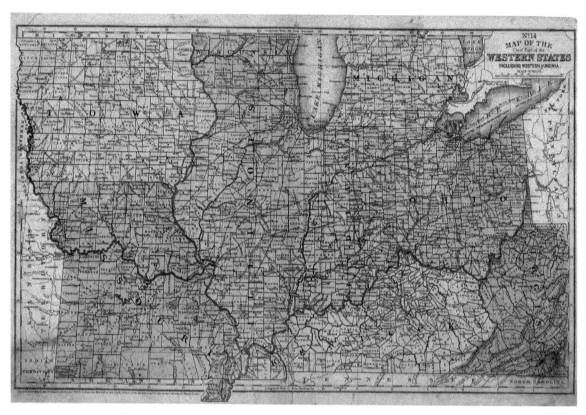

Map of the Chief Parts of the Western States including West Virginia
(Special Collections Department, University of Virginia Library).

Thomas Jeffferson: Archaeologist

FROM AN ALTITUDE OF 29,000 FEET, the face of the trans-Mississippi West has Thomas Jefferson written all over it. In the ever-present gridwork of township and range, section lines and county roads, the land reveals Jefferson's imprint and the lasting presence of his vision. And in the lands beyond St. Louis, it was the Lewis and Clark expedition that brought that vision to the West. This was the vision he expressed in the Land Survey Ordinance of 1784 and repeated in exploration instructions for the Corps of Discovery in 1803. Sweeping up to the Front Range of the Rockies and continuing again to the Pacific, the checkerboard look of the country repeats the Jeffersonian passion for straight lines, tidy corners, and the culture of agriculture. Only in the mountain West is the pattern broken. And even there, given half a chance, the lines and corners will reassert themselves on the land. Few national leaders have made so dramatic and so visible a mark on the American landscape—a landscape fashioned from both earth and imagination. How was it that a Virginian who never traveled west of the Blue Ridge Mountains became so deeply involved in the country beyond the wide Missouri? Why did someone whose own exploring was done eastward across the Atlantic or at home through books and reading launch the first American reconnaissance of the West? And how did it happen that a president determined to have only a modest federal budget should authorize an expensive national scientific enterprise and thus establish a long tradition of government support for exploration and scientific inquiry? William Clark once described Jefferson as "the main spring" of the Corps of Discovery.[1] As the "main spring" he did more than wind up and set in motion the most famous exploring expedition in American history. Out of his own hopes and fears, his travels and reading, Jefferson invented an uniquely American West. Then to mark that West and chart its contours he fashioned an

William Clark by Charles Willson Peale (Independence National Historical Park).

Meriwether Lewis by Charles Willson Peale (Independence National Historical Park).

exploring party led by Meriwether Lewis and William Clark. By joining that traveling company and following its path we make a journey through Jefferson's West.

Something so vast as the western landscape and so compelling as Jefferson's vision for it cannot be grasped at a distance. The bird's eye view, the glimpse from the airplane window, has its value but at so great a height the textures of terrain and life are smoothed out and lost. Jefferson's West calls for close encounters, for views from places like Monticello and St. Louis, Fort Mandan and Fort Clatsop, the Great Falls of the Missouri and the Continental Divide at Lemhi Pass. And if those places offer us latter-day voyagers a spot to watch the journey, paying attention to particular days can fix us to the expedition calendar. Beginning in the middle of the Lewis and Clark story and situating ourselves at the mid-point on the trail we can look back to origins and forward to consequences.

DUTIES OF EMPIRE
THE DAYS OF AUGUST 17, 1805

In mid-July 1805, just as he was preparing to leave humid Washington for a cooler Monticello, Thomas Jefferson received eagerly-anticipated letters and maps from Meriwether Lewis. Drafted during the winter of 1804-5 at Fort Mandan, near present-day Bismarck, North Dakota, the documents gave the president his first detailed accounting of the expedition's progress. Lewis's letter, almost certainly written with an eye toward publication, was filled with plans for the coming year of travel to the Pacific. What the explorer called "the daily detales of our progress" were recorded in Clark's journal, also sent to the president. And most intriguing of all, there was a list of the plant, animal, and ethnographic specimens now on the way east.[2] But it would be on his little mountain, away from politics and personalities, that Jefferson could take the time to grasp just what his captains had found up the Missouri.

Jefferson reached Monticello on July 18 and was soon fully immersed in the daily routines of life on a busy plantation. No matter how arresting the promise of painted buffalo skins, magpies, and prairie dogs, Monticello commanded his first attention. That cargo from the West and Clark's journal would have to wait their turn. By the second week of August he could report that "we are all in good health here, and blest amidst luxuriant crops of every kind."[3] James Madison heard similar news when his friend told him that "we are extremely seasonable in this quarter. better crops were never seen."[4]

On Saturday, August 17, the same day Jefferson wrote to Madison, he once again turned his thoughts to the western expedition. Worried that the recently-arrived botanical and zoological specimens might be damaged through lack of proper care, Jefferson wrote an urgent note to his Washington house manager Etienne Lemaire. "Being apprehensive that the skins and furs may be suffering," Jefferson directed Lemaire to "have them well dried and brushed, and then done up close in strong linen to keep the worm-fly out." In a letter from Lemaire received at Monticello the previous day, Jefferson heard about the magpie and the prairie dog—two western animals collected by Lewis and Clark and now sent to the president. Eager to see them, Jefferson reminded his servant "to have particular care" of the animals "that I may see them alive at my return." But should these western travelers not survive Washington's sweltering summer, the president was especially insistent that the prairie dog's skin and skeleton be preserved. In an enterprise that had already engaged so much of his time and imagination, no detail seemed too small. The matter put right at least on paper, Jefferson the patron of exploration returned to the Saturday duties of Jefferson the planter.[5]

At Monticello August 17 was one more late summer day like countless others. Several thousand miles away, at the forks of the Beaverhead River and Horse Prairie Creek in present-day southwestern Montana, the day was anything but routine. For the Lewis and Clark expedition and the people of Cameahwait's Lemhi Shoshone band, the day was filled with tension, drama, and surprise reunions.

Just four days before, on August 13, Lewis and a small advance party had encountered Cameahwait's people. Now the American travelers and their new Indian friends were at a spot on the east side of the Continental Divide—at a place Lewis later named Camp Fortunate—waiting for Clark and the main body of the expedition to come up the Beaverhead. The explorers' anxious search for horses and a way over the Continental Divide to western waters seemed nearly done. Once over the divide the expedition could confidently make its way to the western rivers that Jefferson and several generations of geographical theorists promised would greet them.

Lewis slept fitfully that Friday night. Worried that Clark's tardy arrival might jeopardize expedition chances to purchase horses and preserve Shoshone good will, Lewis confessed that gloomy thoughts and unsettling fears had crowded his sleep. Early on Saturday morning Lewis ordered George Drouillard, his most experienced scout, and a Shoshone companion to scour the Beaverhead Valley for Clark's party. Some two fretful hours later word came that the main contingent of the Corps of Discovery was making its way through the Beaverhead. The news lifted the tension as everyone—stranger and Shoshone

Thomas Jefferson's Cabinet at Monticello (Thomas Jefferson Foundation, photo by Robert C. Lautman).

alike—was "transplanted with joy." Cameahwait warmly embraced Lewis with what the American explorer had earlier called "the national hug." Camp Fortunate quickly earned its name when Sacagawea recognized a woman who had been with her when both were captured years before by Hidatsa raiders at the Three Forks of the Missouri. The coincidental had happened; now the improbable took place as well. When Sacagawea recognized her brother Cameahwait nearby, the camp took on the appearance of a family reunion.

For all Sacagawea's happiness and Lewis's relief, the real business of the day was yet to come. Once the canoes had been unloaded, Lewis and Clark turned to tasks of diplomacy, geography, and exploration strategy. Those duties stemmed directly from the instructions Jefferson had written some two years before. It was as if the president himself now joined the talk at Camp Fortunate. Late that afternoon the captains, Cameahwait, and several other Shoshones gathered out of the sun under a willow arbor for a grand council. At that moment Camp Fortunate took its place in a long line of diplomatic encounters between native people and European strangers—encounters that began in places with names like Hawikuh, Plymouth, Quebec, and Apalachee. Those were North American places where peoples from many different parts of the world met and struggled to bridge the divide of culture and language. So it was at Camp Fortunate. Sacagawea, Toussaint Charboneau, and François Labiche served as interpreters as each word and phrase moved laboriously from Shoshone to Hidatsa to French to English. As they had done before, Lewis and Clark first "communicated to them [the Shoshones] fully the objects which had brought us into this distant part of the country." But what might have seemed a straightforward idea to Lewis and Clark—the notion of exploration as a national enterprise—was quite foreign to the Shoshones. What did make sense and could narrow the cultural distance was the practice of a trading journey. The Shoshones, like so many other western Indians, took active part in trade networks that spanned the whole continent. And it was the promised benefits of trade that proved common ground. Terrorized by the well-armed Blackfeet and still suffering from a recent Atsina raid, Cameahwait's people saw survival in the shape of American goods and guns. Quick to play that diplomatic card, Lewis and Clark offered firearms in return for horses and a mountain guide. And there was the promise that once the expedition had completed its journey, the traders would come bringing prosperity and security. Cameahwait, whose warrior name meant Black Gun, quickly agreed to the "horses now for guns later" deal.

And to seal the bargain the explorers returned to a ritual that stemmed from more than a century of Anglo-American Indian diplomacy. "Making chiefs" by bestowing peace medals on prominent (and sometimes not-so-prominent) Indians was a predictable part of almost every council, whether in colo-

Reverse of Jefferson's Indian Peace Medal (American Numismatic Society).

nial Pennsylvania or on the edge of Jefferson's western empire. When Lewis and Clark presented Cameahwait and his fellows with medals bearing the likenesses of Washington and Jefferson, the captains' understanding of what they were doing was quite different from that of the Shoshones. Cameahwait and the others likely saw the medals and gifts as signs of respect from one equal to another. Just as they had given the strangers gifts (and in Clark's case, a ceremonial name) the peace medals were appreciated as part of a ritual symbolizing a balanced relationship, a moment of mutual regard. But the medals and the act of giving and receiving them signified something else for the American explorers and the president who sent them. Medals represented sovereignty and national power. Once a chief or headman accepted one, that act was interpreted as acknowledging the sovereign authority of the United States. Cameahwait and the Lemhi Shoshones were no longer "brothers" but "children" bound to respect a distant Great Father.

Obverse of Jefferson's Indian Peace Medal (American Numismatic Society).

Empire and the dreams of an American republic in the West lived inside those bits of round and shiny metal. But such crossed understandings and future controversies seemed far way that Saturday night at Camp Fortunate.

A day that began in joyful reunion and continued with what appeared friendly conversations ended on an unexpectedly worrisome note. Once it was plain that careful negotiating and Sacagawea's presence insured horses for the passage over the Continental Divide, Lewis and Clark pressed Cameahwait for details of the territory ahead. The explorers were still convinced that the waters of the Columbia River and a plain path to the Pacific lay just over the divide in present-day Idaho. This was a fundamental article of faith in Jefferson's hopeful geography, and the expedition had entrusted its future to that gospel. Persuaded that Cameahwait was "a man of Influence Sence and easy and reserved manners," the Americans were ready to pay attention to his geography lesson.

That lesson, with its discouraging description of the road ahead, may not have shattered expedition hopes, but they were surely dented. "The account," Clark admitted, "was verry unfavorable." The river on the west side of the divide (today's Salmon River) "abounded in emence falls, one particularly much higher than the falls of the Missouri." And it was not only the course of the river and the close-crowding mountains that threatened the journey. Cameahwait told Lewis and Clark that the lands to the west and north had neither sufficient game for food nor wood for canoes. Understated as always, Clark drily commented that "this information if true is alarming."[6] At Monticello Jefferson spent part of the day worried lest he not see a magpie and a prairie dog alive. Far from the world of bearded strangers and edgy Shoshones, Jefferson considered expedition science. In what came to be the American West, his captains worried about the arts of survival.

Visions of Empire

Looking back over Jefferson's life and the life of the expedition he set in motion, it might seem that what he and his explorers were doing that Saturday was the logical culmination of years spent studying the West and pondering its future. It is easy to imagine that Thomas Jefferson was always interested in the lands west of the Blue Ridge. He once grandly described himself as "a savage of the mountains."[7] Perhaps no one had read more about the lands beyond St. Louis than Jefferson. And he confessed to John Adams that Indians had fascinated him from "the very early part of my life."[8] Every textbook account of his presidency pays proper attention to the Louisiana Purchase and the Lewis and Clark expedition. But the present has a way of simplifying the past, of giving importance to one path while ignoring others. Thomas Jefferson's road to the West was neither simple nor direct. It is easy to forget that the expedition was planned well before the Louisiana Purchase was undertaken. What led the president and the Corps of Discovery to that August day in 1805 and beyond is a story filled with as many twists and turns as a mountain trail.

By education and temperament Thomas Jefferson faced east. His chosen roads—whether he traveled them as a diplomat, politician, or tourist—led him to places like Philadelphia, Paris, and London. Despite his high-flown rhetoric about republican simplicity and rural virtue, it was the intellectual and physical pleasures of "high culture" that most attracted him. Yet for all the delights of French wine, English gardens, and Italian architecture, there was a moment—a rather long and important moment—when Jefferson left his main-travelled eastern roads and in the mind's eye walked west. What he saw, what he imagined, and what he set in motion changed the history of the North America.

For Jefferson and other Virginians of his generation there was not one West but many Wests—each representing challenge and opportunity, adventure and advancement. Jefferson grew up hearing about his father's West, the country of the Piedmont surveyed and mapped by Peter Jefferson and his fellow adventurer

Joshua Fry in 1749. And there were stories about other Virginia explorers recounted by school master James Maury. By the time of the American Revolution the West meant what is now Ohio, Indiana, and Illinois. This was the West that George Rogers and Clark and his intrepid Virginians seized from the British in 1778. And Jefferson's West grew yet again after the American Revolution. In 1784 his committee report on the temporary government of newly-acquired western lands was the foundation for the Land Ordinances of 1784 and 1785—legislation that forever changed the face of the American landscape. As Washington's secretary of state Jefferson confronted repeated crises involving the Mississippi River and the presence of the great European powers in North America. Throughout the 1780s, thanks in large part to voracious reading, Jefferson gradually expanded his geographic sense of the West as a country beyond the Mississippi, one that reached out to the Pacific and southwest to Santa Fe and New Spain.

If Jefferson's West had once been the Ohio country, now it was the lands watered by the Mississippi and especially the Missouri. This was the West he dimly saw and described in *Notes on the State of Virginia*. Many Virginians, especially land-hungry war veterans, responded eagerly to the promise of a widening West. Families like the Clarks settled in Kentucky, while others perhaps eyed lands beyond St. Louis. Watching that swelling tide of Americans move west, one Spanish official watched and worried. "A new and independent power has now arisen on our continent. Its people are active, industrious, and aggressive. It would be culpable negligence on our part not to thwart their schemes for conquest."[9] Despite that swirl of Spanish worry and American westering, Thomas Jefferson remained firmly set in his eastern orbit, fixed in patterns and obligations more Atlantic than Pacific. Any change would come slowly, prompted more by the bold decisions and actions of others than by his own.

At first glance it may appear that Jefferson became what historian Donald Jackson called "the most towering westerner of his time" more by accident and circumstance than by grand design and personal initiative.[10] And the accidents and circumstances that buffeted North America at the end of the eighteenth century were powerful forces prompting and shaping Jefferson's western days. When he did pause to consider the West, Jefferson was a responsive thinker and statesman, reacting to changing situations rather than seeking to initiate new lines of action or inquiry. Beginning in the early 1780s, Jefferson began to pay close attention to the west beyond the Mississippi. What drew him were specific events he gradually perceived as challenges to a West that might someday be part of the United States.

The modern obsession with instant communication can easily make us over-emphasize what seems the slow pace of the spread of news and information in the late eighteenth century. But in Jefferson's world, news, gossip, and rumor traveled quickly by letter, newspaper, and word of mouth. In late 1783 Jefferson heard a rumor that both piqued his curiosity and drew his concern. Word had it that a group of British entrepreneurs had "subscribed a very large sum of money for exploring the country from the Missisipi to California." And to make matters worse, Jefferson was persuaded that "they pretend it is only to promote knolege." But Jefferson thought he knew better, claiming that the British aimed at colonizing the West. That rumor did have some basis in fact. Traders like Peter Pond, Alexander Henry the Elder, and others associated with the expansionist-minded North West Company were busy building a fur trade empire west of Lake Winnipeg and as far north as the Great Slave Lake. And Pond, ever the visionary explorer and cartographer, had even proposed the possibility of finding the fabled northwest passage. Such a passage could bring Canadian furs to China, and China's wealth to Montreal and Quebec. How Jefferson heard about such schemes remains unclear, but he soon began talking with Virginia friends about some sort of American response. "I am afraid," he wrote George Rogers Clark, that the British "have some thoughts of colonising into that quarter." And it was to Clark, the best-known frontiersman and adventurer of the day, that he turned for advice and leadership. The two already had a lively correspondence about western matters, Clark sending Jefferson seeds, plants, and news about the recently-discovered mastodon bones at Big Bone Lick, Kentucky.

Admitting that his efforts were at best "feeble," Jefferson hoped to persuade Clark to lead an expedition "to search that country."[11] Here in December 1783 was the first real sign of Jefferson's growing concern about a revitalized British Empire in the West. It was a concern that would grow by fits and starts over the next twenty years. As for George Rogers Clark, now deep in debt and sliding toward alcoholism, there could be only one answer to Jefferson's offer. He simply could not afford either the time or the expense such a journey would demand. But in replying to Jefferson, Clark raised a crucial issue—one that Jefferson would be compelled to face two decades later. Who would pay for the comprehensive exploration of the West?[12] Such a vast and expensive enterprise plainly required government funding. No individual, company, American state or even scientific association could afford to launch so risky a venture. Spain, France, and Great Britain had already made geographic exploration a national priority with funds from royal treasuries. Would that strategy fit the needs of a young and relatively poor republic?

Nothing substantial came of Jefferson's overture to Clark. But it was a moment when Jefferson did consider the West and what the new American nation might do if half the continent slipped into the hands of London and Montreal. A West in the hands of a weak Spain was one thing; the presence of Great Britain or France beyond the Missouri meant something very different. Three years later Jefferson was far away from the West, both in geography and daily routine. Spending his days in Paris as ambassador to the court of Versailles, Jefferson was busy exploring salons, bookstalls, and gardens. Despite the social, intellectual, and gastronomic delights of Paris, the American West kept intruding on Jefferson's mind and imagination. Haunting the Paris bookstalls, Jefferson added important travel and exploration accounts to his ever-expanding library. Perhaps it was this reading that made him pay special attention when he heard that the French government was planning a maritime expedition to the Northwest coast of North America. Anxious to know details of the proposed voyage, he employed Revolutionary War naval hero John Paul Jones to uncover French intentions. As fortune had it, the Jean-François de Lapérouse expedition was bound for the South Pacific, but Jefferson's concern about any European nation establishing itself in the West seemed still alive.[13] But what was alive was more worry than plan, more vague fear than any real strategy for exploration.

The West grew a bit larger and a bit more fascinating when Jefferson became involved with the star-crossed adventurer John Ledyard. Like John Paul Jones, Ledyard was part of an informal ambassadorial household establishment

Jefferson inherited from his predecessor Benjamin Franklin. Ledyard was one of those extraordinary young Americans who had already seen much of the world. As a corporal in the Royal Marines, he had been on board HMS *Resolution* with Captain James Cook's third (1776-1780) Pacific voyage of discovery. That voyage took Ledyard from the Northwest coast of America to China, and in the process fired his imagination with dreams about a trade in furs between western North America and the Chinese entrepot at Canton. In letters to Jefferson and Great Britain's Sir Joseph Banks, Ledyard's mind bubbled with all sorts of schemes and ventures. All he lacked was money and a powerful patron.

Intrigued by Ledyard's determination and conviction, Jefferson offered him funds and personal support for a journey of trade and discovery. Ledyard's trek across Siberia, his expulsion by Russian authorities, and eventual death in North Africa on another grand escapade are the stuff of legends. But Ledyard's idea of a North American crossing—hardly unique to him—would not let Jefferson alone. There was something tantalizing and vaguely romantic about an American accompanied only by his dog making his solitary way across the vast continent. As Jefferson explained to the Rev. James Madison in 1788, if the Siberia venture did not succeed, Ledyard might "go to Kentuckey, and endeavor to penetrate Westwardly from thence to the South Sea."[14]

The aborted journeys of George Rogers Clark and John Ledyard had their moments but they never deeply engaged Jefferson's mind and imagination. The same could not be said for the proposal of French naturalist and adventurer André Michaux. Michaux came to America in 1785, seemingly just one more in a long line of scientist-explorers eager to study the New World. Sometime in 1792, after several years of successful botanizing, Michaux approached the American Philosophical Society with a western exploration scheme. Michaux proposed a scientific and commercial journey up the Missouri, across what modest mountains most geographers thought the West might hold, and then on to the Pacific. Michaux's exploration strategy was hardly new. As early as 1673 the French explorers Fr. Jacques Marquette and Louis Jolliet suggested the Missouri River as the most promising highway into the West. In his *Notes on the State of Virginia,* Jefferson described the Missouri as the "principal river" of the western country, reaching deep into the lands beyond St. Louis.[15] Timing is everything, and Michaux came at just the right time for Jefferson and the American Philosophical Society. Jefferson had grown increasingly apprehensive about the prospects of some European nation planting settlements in the West. And the American Philosophical Society was maturing into the primary center for science in the new republic. As the society's energetic vice-president, Jefferson took it on himself to advance Michaux's cause.

More than two decades of reading exploration history taught Jefferson that successful voyages of discovery needed two things—reliable funding and comprehensive instructions. But the notion of the new federal government as Michaux's financial patron seemed out of the question. Instead, begging letters went out to society members, including George Washington. Jefferson himself pledged a small amount, a sum still partly unpaid at his death. But it was the second self-imposed task that proved more important. Journeys such as the one Michaux contemplated required careful planning. Explorers needed the guidance offered by well-crafted instructions. There were few things Jefferson enjoyed more than organizing unruly reality into neat lines and paragraphs. Jefferson understood that exploration was a carefully planned endeavor and he soon set about writing guidelines for such an enterprise.[16]

In a detailed letter to Michaux at the end of April, 1793, Jefferson made plain his geographic vision of the West and what the explorer might accomplish. That vision came about not as the result of western travel experience, but of broad and deep reading. And as always, the journeys that Thomas Jefferson took in his mind were the most important he ever made. As Jefferson understood it, Michaux had one key mission—to find "the shortest and most convenient route of communication between the United States and the Pacific ocean." This was the age-old dream of a northwest passage, a passage that Jefferson and other eighteenth-century geographers moved around the map to suit personal and national desires. Neither Jefferson nor Michaux nor anyone else doubted that such a passage existed and that the Missouri was the key into and through the West. But for all his focus on the Missouri as the key river for the West, Jefferson did not expect Michaux to cross the continent wearing intellectual blinders. The Virginian was a fully modern exploration planner, one inspired by the voyages of Captain James Cook and his patron Sir Joseph Banks. Once on his way to the Pacific, Michaux was to "take notice of the country you pass through."[17] In this, Jefferson showed a keen appreciation for the difference between discovery and exploration. He hoped that Michaux would discover a water passage most European geographers believed already existed. In the process of making that journey of discovery Michaux would also probe and explore the country surrounding the passage. Unlike many of his contemporaries, Jefferson grasped the significance of both a goal-oriented journey and the value of the journey itself. Jefferson's notion of "taking notice" meant making observations of everything from landform and climate to plants and animals new to European science. And Michaux was not to ignore native peoples and cultures, adding descriptions of them to his already bulging notebooks. Jefferson was persuaded that the West was nature's wonderland, holding all sorts of marvels including volcanos, llamas, and the fabled mammoth. A decade earlier, when Jefferson and others fretted about Canadians in the West, they admitted to George Rogers Clark that their efforts had been ineffective. But now Jefferson had moved well beyond that stage, fashioning a comprehensive set of guidelines for an ambitious journey of discovery and exploration.

The instructions prepared for Michaux asked a great deal from one traveler. In his imagination, Jefferson pictured Michaux like Ledyard, making his lonely way west. For all his study of exploration literature, Jefferson still did not quite grasp the true size and scale required for an effective continental reconnaissance. In the age of scientific exploration, useful journeys called for a whole company of travelers. Despite all its promising beginnings, the Michaux expedition never got beyond its first steps west. Caught up in intrigues spawned by the French Revolution, Michaux abandoned his journey in Kentucky and eventually returned to France. Failure is sometimes more productive than success. The American Philosophical Society did not get the geographic and scientific information its members sought, but the Michaux venture did provide Jefferson his first opportunity to be at the very center of exploration planning. In so many ways the Michaux enterprise was Jefferson's apprenticeship in the business of exploration. Ten years later, as he drafted instructions for Meriwether Lewis, Jefferson revisited the Michaux document and found ideas and whole sentences worth reviving.

Jefferson's own explorations took him to England, Italy, and France. Those were the places he came to know by personal experience and direct observation. But the vast interior of North America was no less real to him just because he had not set foot on it. Jefferson's travels in the West were made by way of the printed page and the engraved map. He journeyed with the mind's eye, fashioning his own image of the West built on what others saw and he hoped for. Jefferson's reading mixed with his dreams for an American future, making him a visionary explorer.

Washington on the Potomac was not the place to spend a pleasant summer. Hot, humid days and the threat of political bickering made the seat of government a place to flee from—and Jefferson made sure he spent his presidential summers at Monticello. The summer of 1802 was no exception. Worried by growing tensions with both Spain and France and harried by squabbles with a restive Congress, Jefferson found solace on the mountain with his books. And one of the books ordered from his New York supplier James Cheetham was the recently-published *Voyages from Montreal,* written by the Canadian fur trade explorer Alexander Mackenzie. The book was Mackenzie's account of two (1789, 1792-3) epic voyages in search of a water route across the continent. The second of those journeys took Mackenzie and his party to the Pacific; in July 1793 the Canadians reached the Pacific. Once there, Mackenzie painted his name and the bold words "from Canada, by land, the twenty-second of July, one thousand seven hundred and ninety-three" on a rock in Dean Channel. Some fifteen years later, in early December 1805, a traveler from Jefferson's republic would make a similar gesture. On a tree near the mouth of the Columbia River that adventurer carved the words "William Clark, December 3RD, 1805, by land from the U. States in 1804 & 1805." As fate would have it, the Mackenzie expedition missed linking up with a survey party from the Vancouver expedition by just seven weeks. Had that connection been made, it would have been even more compelling evidence for Britain's advantage in the struggle for empire in the far West. It was now plain that the British posed a real threat to any thoughts Jefferson might have for an American West.

✱ Clark was the one leaving his name —

By modern standards *Voyages from Montreal* is hardly compelling reading. It is a slow-moving narrative with few moments of drama and adventure. But an exciting plot and memorable characters were not what Jefferson looked to find in exploration narratives. What he sought was reliable, useful geographic and scientific information. And Mackenzie seemed to have plenty of that. Jefferson knew about the book as early as January 1802 and was eager to read it. What he found in Mackenzie's account was what he sought, and more. That unexpected extra jolted him wide awake and into action. The final paragraphs of the book contained a remarkable plan for a full-scale British commercial and settlement empire in the West. In those last sections Mackenzie shifted from being a traveler in the employ of a fur company to the role of a remarkably far-sighted empire builder. What Mackenzie proposed was nothing less than an expanded British Empire in North America, one that now included much of the West. And this was to be no mere fur trade domain. Mackenzie envisioned agricultural colonies in the fertile lands south of the Columbia River with that waterway providing an ideal link to world markets. The British and their Canadian friends might have suffered the loss of the Atlantic colonies, but here was a grand opportunity to let the lion stretch once again in North America.[18] What Jefferson heard second- or third-hand about British western aspirations in 1783, he now read in print on paper. His response now could be anything but "feeble." What became the Lewis and Clark expedition might have been born at that moment.

From the vantage point of nearly two centuries it may seem as if Jefferson's decision to launch an American expedition to counter the British threat was yet another example of his responsive thinking about the West. Each one of his western initiatives seemed a response to someone else's idea or enterprise. But when the president told Spanish ambassador Carlos Martínez de Yrujo in December 1802 that he was considering a modest "literary" expedition to the Pacific, more was in hand and at stake than a simple answer to the Mackenzie challenge. *Voyages from Montreal* was the spark, but the fuel had been gathering for more than two decades.

Jefferson's Geography

The story of the Lewis and Clark Expedition has often been written as a story of physical adventure, the tale of courage and hardship in "The Great Unknown." But what made the journey possible and gave it energy and direction were ideas, dreams, and sometimes half-spoken fears. Ignoring the ideas behind the expedition drains much of the life and meaning from it. This was a journey driven by conjectures and speculations about physical geography and natural history, the past of humankind, and the future of the American republic.

Like so many of his contemporaries, Jefferson envisioned human societies as living organisms moving through distinct life stages. As with plants and animals, human communities had moments of birth, childhood, adult life, and a time of decay and death. This cycle was both inevitable and fully consistent with what appeared to be the unchanging laws of Nature. Many eighteenth-century social theorists believed that there were four distinct stages in this bio-cultural cycle. Humankind began as hunters, wedded to what was commonly called "the chase." This was, so European writers imagined, life at its simplest, least civilized, and perhaps most savage. From hunting, humans advanced to tending flocks of sheep and herds of cattle. And at some point some but not all those peoples made the leap forward to become farmers. Eventually, so many predicted, all would come to live in cities and pursue urban—perhaps even industrial—ways. Writing long after the return of the Corps of Discovery, Jefferson offered his own vivid picture of human social change as seen through the eyes of an explorer. "Let a philosophic observer commence a journey from the savages of the Rocky Mountains, eastwardly towards our sea-coast. These he would observe in the earliest stage of association living under no law but that of nature, subscribing and covering themselves with the flesh and skins of wild beasts. He would next find those on our frontiers in the pastoral state, raising domestic animals to supply the defects of hunting. Then succeed our own semi-barbarous citizens, the pioneers of the advance of civilization, and so in his progress he would meet the gradual shades of improving man until he would reach his, as yet, most improved state in our seaport towns. This, in fact, is equivalent to a survey, in time, of the progress of man from the infancy of creation to the present day."[19] While some writers saw the process as equally inevitable and beneficial, others were alarmed by the prospect of the American republic as a nation of cities and town-dwellers.

Jefferson embraced the evolutionary scheme of social development with its judgements about progress and civilization, but at the same time he was deeply troubled about the prospect of the American republic destined to abandon rural ways for urban life. Few ideas were more fundamental to his vision of the American future than the bond between republican virtue and the rural life. As he famously said to John Jay in 1785: "Cultivators of the earth are the most valuable citizens. They are the most vigorous, the most independent, the most virtuous, and they are tied to their country and wedded to its liberty and interests by the most lasting bonds."[20] And writing two years later to James Madison, Jefferson was even more direct. "I think our governments will remain virtuous for many centuries; as long as they are chiefly agricultural; and this will be as long as there shall be vacant lands in any part of America. When they get piled upon one another in large cities, as in Europe, they will become corrupt as in Europe."[21] Committed to the connection between republican virtues and an agricultural society, Jefferson believed that city life would doom the American experiment. Somehow the nation had to be kept in a perpetual state of rural simplicity and economic self-sufficiency. It was as if the whole social aging process might be held at bay. At the same time Jefferson recognized that American farmers were part of a global market place. Economic self-sufficiency did not mean isolation. As he explained to his Dutch correspondent G. K. van Hogendorp, Americans "have a decided taste for navigation and commerce."[22] Simply put, the spirit of commercial enterprise was already a part of the life of the republic. The theory of a self-sufficient farming community living in splendid republican isolation was just that—a theory. Jefferson knew it and admitted it. No prudent politician could afford to ignore the commercial spirit of the age. The best Jefferson could hope for might be to fashion a commercial nation with an export economy based on agriculture. Such a vision of the national future required two elements—vast

Related to the farm bills of today.

supplies of fertile land and a reliable transportation system linking American farms to global markets. Profit-minded Americans would not stay on the farm unless there was the promise of profit. And those financial rewards would come only if good land and access to markets seemed within reach. The price of continued republican virtue, so it seemed, had to be measured in land and rivers. Give the sons and daughters of 1776 those things, and the future would be secure. In so many ways the Lewis and Clark expedition was all about finding and mapping those farm-to-market highways and evaluating the fertility of the western garden. If the West was to fulfill Jefferson's vision of a ever-youthful republic, Lewis and Clark had to find a useful passage through it and to the busy world beyond.

For all its promise, the West did not have an unclouded future. Buried deep within the colonial experience was the lasting fear of being surrounded by enemies both spiritual and corporeal. From the earliest beginnings at Jamestown and Plymouth, English settlers were beset by fears of being surrounded, encircled by European rivals and hostile native neighbors. And this was no idle fear. For nearly two centuries the English colonies had been virtually surrounded by French, Spanish, and Native American foes. Perhaps it was inevitable that American expansionists like Jefferson should inherit this colonial, coastal perspective.

And in the summer of 1802 the vision of a republic surrounded and in peril seemed all too real. From the Ohio country to the Southeast, native nations were a formidable presence. To the North, thanks to visionaries like Pond and Mackenzie, there seemed a revitalized British Empire with designs on the West. And already firmly in place on the Pacific coast and in the greater Southwest, Spain was a presence no one could safely ignore. But perhaps what troubled Jefferson most that summer was the threat of Napoleon and the return of France in America. Just a year before, in May 1801, there was word of the Treaty of San Ildefonso and the retrocession of a vast part of the continent to France. Louisiana—however defined—seemed destined to be part of a greater France. And French Louisiana would stand as an impenetrable barrier keeping the United States hemmed in to an Atlantic future. Denied the West and its fertile lands, the American future would be grim. Little wonder that reading Mackenzie jolted the president into action. Perhaps Napoleon's imperial schemes could not be stopped, but at least the American nation could match Mackenzie's imperial journey with one of its own.[23]

In late November 1802 Jefferson took the Spanish ambassador Carlos Martínez de Yrujo aside for what the diplomat described as talk "in a frank and confident tone." Knowing that the Corps of Discovery would have to pass through Spanish territory, Jefferson was eager to allay any fears of invasion and conquest. Describing the expedition as "a small caravan" intent on "the advancement of geography," Jefferson admitted to the ambassador that the official purpose of the journey would be cast in commercial terms since the Constitution did not grant Congress power to appropriate funds for a "purely literary" journey. Martínez was not taken in by Jefferson's slippery words, reporting that the expedition was plainly an effort "to discover the way by which the Americans may some day extend their population and their influence up to the coasts of the South Sea."[24] But that phrase—"the advancement of geography"—was intriguing. It was Jefferson's acknowledgement that systematic scientific inquiry had become an essential part of any exploration venture. Inspired by the voyages of captains James Cook and George Vancouver as well as the role of Sir Joseph Banks and the Royal Society, Jefferson made natural history one of the proposed expedition's many missions. An active citizen of the republic of science, Jefferson hoped that his explorers would enlarge and enrich the kingdom of the mind. And like Banks, Jefferson saw a direct connection between exploration, the advancement of science, and the expansion of empire.

Jefferson's use of the word "geography" in his conversation with the Spanish ambassador was another clue about the relationship between the proposed western expedition and the president's own conception of the western landscape. If the central mission of the expedition was to locate a Jeffersonian version of the northwest passage, then that mission was built on a particular conception of the physical geography of North America. Like his fellow American geographers— Jefferson was a geographer in the broadest sense—the Virginian saw the landscape in terms of balance and symmetry. The mountains and rivers on the western side of the continent must surely be similar to those on the eastern side. The Rocky or Stony Mountains were certain to be like the Applachians—heavily timbered and blessed with many passes and water gaps. In *Notes on the State of Virginia*, Jefferson graded rivers on their prospects as avenues for commerce.[25] Navigability was more important than scenic splendor. Jefferson fashioned western rivers in the image of the Potomac, the Ohio, and the Mississippi. These eastern rivers were notable for their navigability, a role they might play as highways for commerce and empire. Western rivers, so Jefferson reasoned, must also be navigable. And the headwaters for rivers like the Missouri and the Great River of the West (a phrase often used to describe the Columbia) were bound to be close to each other just opposite of a narrow ridge or height of land. When Jefferson explained his notions about western rivers and their role in a northwest passage to French naturalist Bernard Lacépède, his correspondent quickly grasped the idea. "If your nation," wrote Lacépède, "could establish an easy communication route by river, canal and short portages, between New York, for example, and the town which would be built at the mouth of the Columbia, what a route that would be for trade from Europe, from Asia, and from America, whose northern products would arrive at this route by the Great Lakes and the upper Mississippi, while the southern products of the New World would arrive there by the lower Mississippi and by the Rio Norte of New Mexico, the source of which is near the 40th parallel! What greater means to civilization than these new communication routes!"[26] Jefferson never thought that a single river channel ran through all of North America. Like Lacépède, he had in mind a much more complex geography that encompassed rivers, canals, trails, and portages. This was an imperial geography, one based on unequal measures of reliable knowledge and optimistic faith.

The West was sure to be like the East not only in mountains and rivers but in land quality as well. The image of America as a garden was centuries old by Jefferson's time. What had begun as an artistic and literary device emerged by the end of the eighteenth century as a model for social planning. Considering his faith in an agricultural republic, Jefferson's conception of the garden centered on plants more useful than ornamental. His garden in the West would be planted with corn, beans, and wheat. Although a child of the tobacco South, Jefferson's western garden looked more like the farms of Pennsylvania or southern New England.

Whatever its precise outlines, Jefferson was persuaded that the land beyond St. Louis was a rich and fertile country.

All this conjecture added up to a compelling geography of hope. And it was something more as well. This was an American teleology, one that saw the future written on the very face of the earth. Present as early as Jamestown and Plymouth, this mixture of geography, nationalism, and land hunger culminated in the passionate rhetoric of the 1840s known as Manifest Destiny. Desire created reality. And it was desire, writes Barry Lopez, that "causes imagination to misconstrue what it finds."[27] The terrain that would make possible Jefferson's cherished "empire of liberty" was there in the West because it had to be. Jefferson's faith would make it so. The travel strategy laid out for André Michaux and Lewis and Clark was built on those very ideas. What historical geographer John L. Allen has called "the passage through the American garden" would take Jefferson's explorers up the Missouri, over the Rockies by an easy portage, and down the Great River of the West to the Pacific.[28] The way West had already been marked out by Nature; all Lewis and Clark had to do was find the grand highway.

The grand enterprise we know as the Lewis and Clark expedition began to take identifiable shape in the spring of 1803. What had been sparked by reading Alexander Mackenzie was now fanned to flame by growing fears over French designs on North America. Unaware that Napoleon had decided to abandon his Louisiana dream and offer the country to American buyers, Jefferson began the task of expedition planning. And the most fundamental task was the careful preparation of exploration instructions. While the selection of his private secretary Meriwether Lewis to lead the western tour was a crucial decision, the whole journey depended on writing a document that would guide the explorers in their daily duties. The very idea of fashioning the journey by means of a document appealed to someone who, so a recent biographer has written, believed that "making public policy was essentially a textual problem."[29] In telling his explorers what to search out, Jefferson was inventing his own version of the West. Writing about the West meant making it. The instructions for Lewis were an expression of what Jefferson believed his captains would see and experience on their journey. If the text guiding the expedition was sufficiently rigorous and comprehensive, results would be assured. By temperament and legal training, Jefferson was drawn to the question-and-answer form of inquiry and explanation. His only book, *Notes on the State of Virginia*, was composed in response to a questionnaire and preserved something of that form in its chapters. Little wonder that the instructions prepared for Meriwether Lewis came as a series of questions. At first glance the sentences in the instructions appear as declarative statements. But Jefferson meant them as questions, categories of inquiry. Like him, we might think of explorers as questioners, inquiring their way into a strange country.

While Jefferson had the Michaux instructions as a kind of first draft, it was plain to him that the enterprise now in mind was larger and more complex. As Donald Jackson writes, "It is no longer useful to think of the Lewis and Clark expedition as the personal story of two men. Their journey was an enterprise of many aims and a product of many minds."[30] No one appreciated the need for many minds more than Jefferson himself. Sometime in early April 1803 he completed an initial instructions draft and circulated it among cabinet officers. Just as he had already asked the Philadelphia scientific community to advise Lewis on matters of natural history, so now he sought help from friends and colleagues closer to home. What Jefferson sent was probably a document much like the Michaux directions—specific enough on the core mission of a passage to the Pacific but lacking in additional details. And some of what was missing prompted valuable replies from unexpected sources.

Secretary of State James Madison had often written about territorial expansion and the future of the republic. In *The Federalist Papers* (especially Number 10) Madison suggested territorial expansion as the ideal way to dilute political factionalism. But for reasons that remain unclear, the proposed western expedition did not capture the secretary's imagination. Already of one mind on an American empire in the West, perhaps Madison saw little reason to comment on this preliminary draft. His sparse comments appear to have added little to Jefferson's final version.[31] The important responses came from what might seem to us unexpected quarters—the Department of the Treasury and the office of the Attorney-General. Like Jefferson, Treasury Secretary Albert Gallatin was a polymath. His interests ranged from public finance and international diplomacy to comparative linguistics and ethnography. Gallatin's April 13 letter displayed his usual grasp of the imperial conflicts that shaped the history of the entire continent. In an observation remarkable for its prescience and brass-knuckle realism, Gallatin urged the president to be prepared to occupy Louisiana by force if necessary lest the British do so first. While Jefferson was unwilling on paper or in public to directly link the expedition to territorial expansion, Gallatin had no such qualms. He took the connection as obvious and necessary. "The future destinies of the Missouri country," Gallatin emphasized, "are of vast importance to the United States, it being perhaps the only large tract of country, and certainly the first which lying out of the boundaries of the Union will be settled by the people of the U. States." Even if the party failed to reach the Pacific—an eventuality Gallatin chose to ignore—the journey up the Missouri and to the base of the Rockies was sure to provide valuable information. And Gallatin was certain that the Missouri country would be the heart of Jefferson's self-renewing republic. As he said, "the great object to ascertain is whether from its extent and fertility that country is susceptible of a large population, in the same manner as the corresponding tract on the Ohio." That word "Ohio" meant more than one place or one river on the map. It was a kind of cultural shorthand for fertile lands of great promise. The very mention of the word "Ohio" connected the West beyond the Mississippi to the Old Northwest of the Ohio country. Embracing Jefferson's conception of western geography, Gallatin quickly grasped the meaning of the journey as an act of national faith.[32]

While the president surely knew about the Treasury secretary's broad understanding of diplomatic and geographic issues, there may have been little to prepare him for Attorney-General Levi Lincoln's comprehensive and valuable reply. Lincoln often advised Jefferson on domestic politics—especially those relating to New England—and he had taken the measure of Meriwether Lewis as well. Most important, Lincoln understood that the expedition was an expression of national policy, one that was sure to have partisan political consequences. "I consider the enterprise," he wrote on April 17, "of national consequence, and, to a degree personally hazardous, to the projectors and individual adventurers." Lincoln was all too aware that Jefferson's opposition in Congress was both vocal and well-organized. Branding the Federalists as "perverse, hostile, and malignant,"

Lincoln asked the obvious but painful question. What should Jefferson and his administration do if the expedition failed to find the passage to the Pacific? Failure, even the slightest hint of failure, would transform the expedition into a political embarrassment and perhaps even a national laughingstock. The instructions draft that Lincoln saw—a document that has not survived—evidently said little about science and ethnography. What the expedition needed, so Lincoln believed, were additional missions as justifications for success should the passage prove as elusive as ever. "Besides," as he cunningly put it, "religion and morality making a very important article in the history of all countries as an object of attention, if the enterprise appears to be an attempt to advance them, it will by many people, on that account, be justified, how calamitous the issue." Squarely facing the possibility of failure in the core mission, Lincoln also suggested caution when drafting orders for Lewis. Lincoln sensed that Lewis could be impetuous, foolhardy, and too ready to place himself and his command in harm's way. Jefferson evidently agreed with all these suggestions, and the final draft has much of Levi Lincoln in it.[33]

What emerged from this collaboration was Jefferson's letter of instructions for Meriwether Lewis. Dated June 20, 1803, it was both the expression and the culmination of Jefferson's thinking about the West, its exploration, and the future of the American republic. Surely one of his most influential state papers, the document became the charter for federal exploration throughout the nineteenth century. Its questions marked out fields of inquiry that would define and guide the journeys of dozens of explorers, cartographers, and scientists. And on the personal level, the instructions for Lewis insured that Jefferson would be on the expedition's journey. It would be his mind and his sensibilities that would inform every decision, every observation, every step of the way West.

And Jefferson did expect that there would be many future voyages of discovery. This first one had a single mission. Jefferson believed in the transforming power of useful knowledge, and the most useful knowledge the Pacific expedition could yield was the route to the western sea. Everything else—all the botany, climatology, and ethnography—was secondary. And to make sure Lewis got the point and did not stray from the goal, Jefferson described the Corps of Discovery's mission in unmistakably blunt terms. "The object of your mission is to explore the Missouri river, and such principal stream of it, as, by it's course and communication with the waters of the Pacific ocean, whether the Columbia, Oregan, Colorado or any other river may offer the most direct and practicable water communication across this continent for the purposes of commerce."[34] In one sentence Jefferson had managed to summarize both his geographic conception of the West and the role of a passage through the garden linking that West to the rest of the world. Six months later, when Lewis and Clark were in St. Louis preparing for the trip west, Lewis offhandedly suggested a brief excursion toward Santa Fe. Jefferson's reply was sharp and quick. "The object of your mission is single, the direct water communication from sea to sea formed by the bed of the Missouri and perhaps the Oregon."[35] The heart of the journey had not changed, but Jefferson had taken Lincoln's advice. Expedition instructions now said much about Indians and science. Those missions were not merely cosmetic, inserted to fend off political attacks. But the dream of the passage and its promise for the future was still at the center of Jefferson's mind and imagination.

The object of the mission was single, but Jefferson the patron of Enlightenment exploration never expected his explorers to march West as if through a mental tunnel. Aware that the journey itself might yield results nearly as important as finding the passage, Jefferson drafted instructions requiring the expedition to pay attention to "the face of the country." Echoing words first used with Michaux, that phrase was meant to encompass everything from plants and animals to weather and terrain. In some ways, the instructions read like a table of contents for an encyclopedia of the American West. Modern students of the Lewis and Clark expedition sometimes fault Jefferson for not sending a more carefully trained scientist on the journey. But Jefferson understood that American scientific exploration had to proceed more slowly than the grand enterprises led by Cook and Vancouver. In an especially astute appraisal of American scientific institutions and the rigors of doing science in the West, Jefferson wrote the following to his correspondent C.F.C. Volney. "These expeditions are so laborious, and hazardous, that men of science, used to the temperature and inactivity of their closet, cannot be induced to undertake them. They are led therefore by persons qualified expressly to give us the geography of the rivers with perfect accuracy, and of good common knolege and observation in the Animal, vegetable, and mineral departments. When the route shall be once open and known, scientific men will undertake, and verify and class it's subjects."[36] Jefferson never claimed that Lewis belonged to the fraternity of "scientific men" but only that the young army officer was a keen naturalist. And natural history, with its techniques of observation, collection, description, and classification, was what Jefferson had in mind. Natural history emphasized useful knowledge, the sort of learning that could be applied to the benefit of humankind. Lewis and Clark could begin the process of gathering such knowledge. Later, "scientific men" would come out of their closets, march West over routes blazed by hardier travelers, and further advance the kingdom of the mind. And Jefferson's vision of science in the West came true. Beginning in the 1820s with the Stephen H. Long expedition, scientists accompanied all major federal exploring enterprises. John C. Frémont, John Wesley Powell, Ferdinand V. Hayden, and many others all made science central to their journeys.

When Thomas Jefferson looked west from Monticello, he did not imagine an empty continent. The West might be a wilderness on the way to becoming an garden, but it was also a place many native people called home. Whatever Jefferson thought about Native Americans—and his thinking was never either fixed or consistent—he knew that Indians would play an essential role in both the Lewis and Clark expedition and all future exploration in the West. Even the most cursory reading of his instructions for Lewis reveals how large Indians loomed in Jefferson's imagination. More than half of the space in the text is taken up with questions relating to some seventeen aspects of Indian life and culture. With his passion for organizing life into orderly tables and columns, perhaps Jefferson imagined the Corps of Discovery might create a cultural and geographic inventory of Native Americans in the West. And in fact, Lewis and Clark did just that in their "Estimates of Eastern and Western Indians." Directing the explorers to enumerate "the names of the nations and their numbers," Jefferson sought information about tribal boundaries, inter-tribal relations, and "peculiarities in their laws, customs, and dispositions." Native life, so Jefferson believed, might also reveal the character of humankind at an earlier stage of social evolution. Jefferson wanted Lewis and Clark to pay attention to Indians' "ordinary occupations in agriculture, fishing, hunting, war, arts, and implements for these." And if there was any time to spare, the president hoped his captains might gather Indian language vocabularies and "what knolege you can of the state of morality, religion, and information among them."[37] This was as complete an agenda as any explorer might have, and it proved to be the guiding force behind much of the ethnography done by the federal government for the rest of the century.

But Jefferson never expected that Indians would be passive subjects for study by his travelers. While not saying so explicitly, he may have understood that exploration was a cooperative enterprise, one that involved both his captains and their native hosts. That cooperative dimension ranged from providing food, shelter, and companionship to important botanical and zoological specimens. Indians would involve themselves in the life of the expedition as interpreters, guides, and cartographers. Among the many minds that shaped the expedition as it made its way west, there were native minds as well. Without Indian partners, the expedition could not succeed.

Over the next two and a half years, from May 1804 to September 1806, the story of Jefferson's West must follow two paths, two journeys. The familiar story traces the Corps of Discovery as it makes it way up the Missouri, across the Rockies, and down the Columbia to the Pacific. And the eastward passage, so often neglected in the telling, has its own tale of hard travel, disappointment, violence, and triumphant return. The less familiar journey is the one Jefferson made in his own imagination as he tracked the expedition, worried about its survival, and pondered its larger consequences. There were certain days over those two and a half years when both the explorers and their patron found themselves pursuing similar or complimentary tasks. Those were the days when discovery and exploration took place both at Monticello or Washington and beyond the wide Missouri. They are the emblematic days that reveal the larger story of Jefferson, the Corps of Discovery, and the West.

Measuring for Empire
The Days of November 15 & 16, 1803

In mid-November 1803 the Corps of Discovery had not even begun to travel what William Clark called "our road across the Continent." Not yet at full strength, the expedition was making its way by river passage to St. Louis. Meriwether Lewis later described the journey from Pittsburgh to Cincinnati as a "most tedious and laborious passage."[38] On November 11 the party pulled up at Fort Massac, overlooking the Ohio River at present-day Metropolis, Illinois. At that army post Lewis and Clark engaged George Drouillard, an able frontiersman of Shawnee and French ancestry. In rain and thunder the explorers made their way toward what all recognized as a key point for American expansion—the confluence of the Ohio and Mississippi rivers. On November 15 the travelers were at the confluence near present-day Cairo, Illinois. Once there, Lewis and Clark paused to measure and map that key river junction. In Jefferson's grand continental geography the Ohio and Mississippi were esential parts of the larger passage. And in terms of national military strategy, few locations east of St. Louis were as important as this river junction. Using a surveyor's compass, Clark calculated the width of the Ohio and made a partial survey of the point of land where the two rivers met. And it was here that the explorers made their first effort to determine latitude and longitude, an enterprise that would occupy and frustrate them for some time to come. To complete these calculations, Clark drew a sketch map of the confluence.[39]

What Lewis and Clark did that day was fundamental to exploration in the Age of Enlightenment. Like their European contemporaries, they were calculating and measuring empire. Exploring and mapping were bound together in a great Enlightenment project—one that English writer Edmund Burke described as unrolling "The Great Map of Mankind." Locating themselves in the landscape, Lewis and Clark were also marking the outlines of an extensive river system that would insure the future of the republic. Writing to Lewis the following day, the

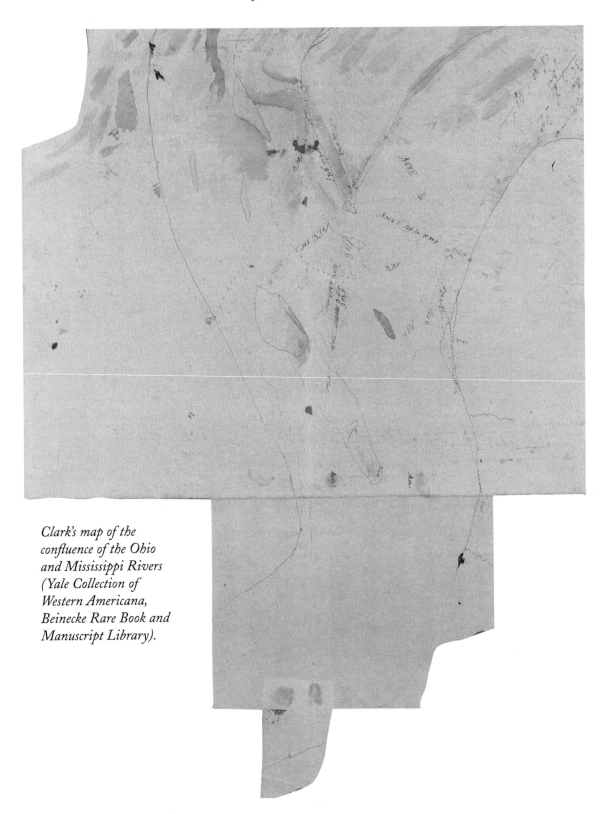

*Clark's map of the
confluence of the Ohio
and Mississippi Rivers
(Yale Collection of
Western Americana,
Beinecke Rare Book and
Manuscript Library).*

president was also busy defining an expanding American empire. Jefferson's letter contained three vital pieces of information: the official "Account of Louisiana", news about the Act of Possession, and extracts from the 1795 journal of Missouri River trader and explorer Jean Baptiste Truteau. It was the information from Truteau that must have seemed most valuable to the president and his explorers. Truteau offered a census and commentary tracing Missouri River tribes from the Mandan, Hidatsa, and Arikara towns to the Crow and Sioux bands. He also knew about the locations and hunting patterns of the Omaha, Otoe, Pawnee, and Osage peoples. But perhaps what pleased Jefferson most was Truteau's observation that "the soil of the Missouri is the most fertile in the universe." And it was also a time to once again remind Lewis and Clark of their central mission. In an earlier letter to Jefferson, Lewis had idly suggested a side-trip toward Santa Fe during the winter of 1803-4. As he put it, "I have concluded to make a tour this winter on horseback of some hundred miles through the most interesting portion of the country adjoining my winter establishment."[40] Jefferson would have none of it. The Lewis and Clark detachment of the Corps of Discovery had one compelling mission. Anything that took the expedition away from that central goal endangered its success and jeopardized Jefferson's larger plans for continental exploration.

And he did have a larger plan in mind. Jefferson's careful study of contemporary exploration taught him the value of several journeys covering large areas. What he had in mind was a comprehensive survey of the rapidly-expanding American empire. As he explained to Lewis, the plan called for three coordinated explorations of the Mississippi, the Missouri, and their tributaries. Lewis and Clark were to head up the Missouri. In 1805 Zebulon Montgomery Pike carried out an reconnaissance of the upper Mississippi. Arranging to explore the lower Mississippi, the Red, and the Arkansas proved a more troublesome task. William Dunbar, Jefferson's correspondent and fellow-naturalist, led a small party up the Ouachita River into present-day Arkansas. But when the president asked him to lead a more extensive survey up the Red River and then down the Arkansas River, Dunbar politely refused. What emerged instead was the Thomas Freeman-Peter Custis expedition of 1806. Freeman was an accomplished surveyor and Custis had some botanical and zoological training. That part of the larger Corps of Discovery was to explore the Red River. Seeing the Freeman-Custis party as an invasion of territory outside the bounds of the Louisiana Purchase, Spanish troops forced the Americans to halt at what is today Bowie County, Texas. Whatever the outcome of these more southern journeys, the idea of three coordinated exploring parties suggests Jefferson's growing sophistication as an exploration planner. In a memorable phrase, Jefferson expected his expanded Corps of Discovery would "fix with precision the contour of our new limits."[41]

Mid-November 1803 was not a time of great decision or high adventure. There were no dramatic encounters with Indians or narrow escapes from disaster. No one today would mark this moment as a turning point for either Jefferson or the Corps of Discovery. But perhaps no other time in the life of the expedition reveals so much about Jefferson's conception of exploration, the ways that conception might be brought to life, and the implications of all this for the future shape of the West. Just as William Clark measured the width of the Ohio River and mapped its confluence with the Mississippi, so Jefferson made large calculations about the new limits of the American republic. Calculation and exploration, possession and occupation—all came together in the late fall of 1803.

DISTANCES OF EMPIRE
THE DAYS OF NOVEMBER 6, 1804

Just a year later, in November 1804, the Lewis and Clark expedition was well along on its road across the continent. In late October the travelers reached the Mandan and Hidatsa villages near present-day Bismark, North Dakota. Clustered around the Knife River confluence with the Missouri, the three Mandan and two Hidatsa villages comprised the most important Indian trading and diplomacy center on the northern Great Plains. Native people from throughout the Great Plains came to exchange horses and leather goods for corn and other foodstuffs. Europeans had made their way to the earth lodge villages as early as the 1730s, and by 1804 traders from Canada and St. Louis were regular visitors on the banks of the Knife. Lewis and Clark would be just one more company of travelers hoping to find Mandan and Hidatsa hospitality. With a combined population greater than that of St. Louis, the Mandan and Hidatsa towns were at the heart of northern plains life. It was there that the Corps of Discovery intended on wintering over before making its final push to the western sea.

In the earliest hours of Tuesday, November 6 the expedition's night sentries had their usually-peaceful guard duty suddenly interrupted when the sky shimmered with the Northern Lights. Awakened by the sergeant of the guard, members of the expedition watched the aurora borealis dance through the darkness. For men who had lived under eastern skies this was an astounding sight. Determined to record the face of the heavens, Clark struggled to find the right words. What he did write captures, despite the troubled syntax, the sense of wonder and awe so many travelers feel when night comes to the northern plains and the sky glows. "A Nothern light, which was light, not red, and appearred to Darken and Some Times nearly obscured, and open, many times appeared in light Streeks, and at other times a great Space light and containing floating Collomns which appeared to approach each other and retreat leaveing the lighter space at no time of the same appearance."[42]

A day beginning in mystery and spectacle soon returned to the ordinary, backbreaking work of building a winter Fort Mandan. Triangular in shape with two ranges of sleeping quarters, a stockade wall and gate, the post represented the first formal American presence on the plains. It was also a new way to define space on the northern plains, not by circles but by straight lines and sharp corners. From here Lewis and Clark would announce the power of the United States, the presence of a new Great Father, and the shape of things to come. But as the wind turned hard and cold from the northwest, it was common work and not diplomacy that filled the expedition's day. There were logs to cut, huts to build, and latrines to dig. And in the midst of that work there was a reminder of the distance that separated the explorers from their patron. In the afternoon a small party led by sometime-interpreter and trader Joseph Gravelines left Fort Mandan for the down river Arikara villages. Gravelines had long been in the Missouri River Indian trade and knew the Arikara language. There they would pick up the Arikara headman Arketarnarshar for a visit with the Great Father in Washington. Organizing Indian delegations was an important part of the expedition's official duties. This particular delegation would not reach Jefferson until April 1806—yet another reminder of the challenges of time and distance posed by the sheer size of the West.[43]

The same day, eastward half a continent away, Thomas Jefferson faced the challenge of distance and the passion to know about events far away. A letter addressed to Meriwether Lewis had come to hand prompting the president to write Lewis's brother Reuben. Here was an opportunity to summarize the expedition's progress and speculate on the explorers' future moves. For all his painstaking efforts at planning the expedition's journey, the president knew little about its daily progress up the Missouri. He could report that the party had passed the Platte River near present-day Omaha, Nebraska on August 4. And remarkably, Jefferson's information about that milestone of the journey was only off the mark by a little less than two weeks, the expedition having reached the Platte on July 21. The president also knew something of the meeting held with the Oto and Missouria Indians and the diplomatic arrangements made with several of the chiefs on August 3.

And there was more. Over the course of their journey, Lewis and Clark formulated several different plans designed to fulfill the many missions laid out in their instructions. Several of those strategies involved dividing the exploring party to best use available resources and personnel. What Jefferson heard and then passed on to Reuben Lewis was one of those schemes. As he understood it, the expedition would winter somewhere up the Missouri. When spring came and ice on the river broke up, half the party would return to St. Louis with the keelboat and its cargo of specimens, journals, and maps. What Lewis and Clark came to call "the permanent party" would head west up the Missouri and toward the mountains. A small group might remain at the winter quarters to raise corn for re-supply on the return journey. What Jefferson heard proved remarkably accurate. In the spring of 1805 Corporal Richard Warfington and a small detachment took the expedition's keelboat back to St. Louis while the rest of the Corps of Discovery pointed toward the Pacific. With food supplies assured from Mandan friends, no one need stay to tend Fort Mandan's gardens. Seeking to reassure Lewis's family of the explorer's safety, Jefferson claimed that all encounters with Indians had been friendly and peaceful. Stretching the truth to fit the occasion, the president declared that Lewis and his companions were as safe in the West as they might have been at home.[44]

If the moment in November 1803 was all about calculation and the quest for certain knowledge, then November 6, 1804 promised mystery and uncertainty. This November day offered a lesson in trying to be in touch and being just out of touch. Here in unmistakable terms was the presence of distance, the awesome power of western space. William Least Heat-Moon, one of the most acute observers of the modern Great Plains, writes this about space and the West: "The true West differs from the East in one great, pervasive, influential, and awesome way: space. Space west of the line is perceptible and often palpable, especially when it appears empty, and it's that apparent emptiness which makes matter look alone, exiled, and unconnected. The terrible distances eat up speed. Even dawn takes nearly an hour just to cross Texas."[45] Jefferson and Lewis and Clark could not escape the uncertainties imposed by western distances. Once so sure about the expedition, its missions, and the nature of the West in his confident-sounding instructions, the president could only sound certain about the explorers' future travel plans. And the magical Northern Lights? Like the Indians preparing to explore the new nation's capital and the country beyond, the Corps of Discovery was witness to things invisible, remote, real but beyond reach.

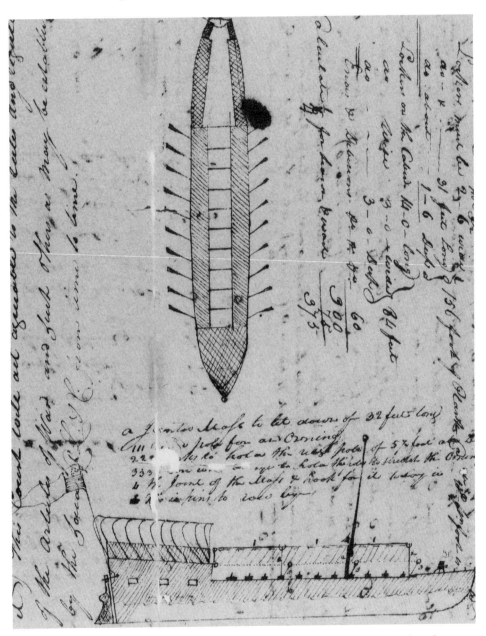

Keelboat and pirogue from Clark's field notes (Yale Collection of Western Americana, Beinecke Rare Book and Manuscript Library).

Picturing Empire
The Days of May 25, 1805

An experienced St. Louis merchant once described any voyage up the Missouri in a single word—"toilsome."[46] In late May 1805 the Lewis and Clark expedition was learning firsthand the truth of that observation. Struggling against a powerful spring rise, expedition boatmen spent long hours in waist-high water or on slippery river banks hauling heavily-loaded perogues and canoes. There was nothing grand or romantic about this kind of exploration; it was work that exhausted the strongest among them. On May 25 the expedition was on the Missouri in present-day Fergus County, Montana, deep in what are known as the Missouri Breaks. Sergeant Patrick Gass thought the country looked like "great heaps of clay, washing away with every shower; with scarcely any herbs or grass on any of them."[47]

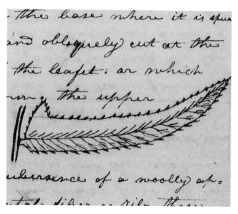

Christmas fern from Lewis's journal (American Philosophical Society).

That day the work became even more arduous as the wind shifted around to blow directly against the travelers. Progess now was even slower and more painful. Lewis admitted in his journal entry for the day that the combination of wind and current "compelled us to double our force" in order to make any headway.

Discovery and exploration on these days promised only backbreaking, straining labor that measured the course of empire in aching muscles and bruised feet. But on this weary day Jefferson's letter of exploration instructions was much in evidence. For all the toil up the Missouri, Lewis did not forget his role as the expedition's naturalist. The Bighorn sheep had only recently become known to European science. Throughout the day Lewis observed what he described as "gangs of the big-horned Anamals on the face of the steep bluffs and clifts."

Admiring their fine form and surefootedness, Lewis ordered Drouillard to shoot one so that it could be more closely examined. Clark and William Bratton, also on shore reconnoitering the country, shot an additional two bighorns.

That night in camp, while others rested after a demanding day, Lewis set to work drafting a finely-detailed word portrait of the bighorn. Revealing his sensitive eye for shape and color, Lewis described this animal in masterful detail. He hardly missed a feature—head, hair, legs, rump, and those remarkable toes. Like an artist, Lewis shaded his big horn painting in tones of brown, black, green, and silver. He counted the teeth, compared the hair coat to the antelope, and noted the many uses native people made of the horn. Lewis also placed the animal in its habitat. It was where the bighorn lived and how it moved that drew Lewis's obvious admiration. "The places they gerally celect to lodg is the cranies and cevices of the rocks in the faces of inacessable precepices, where the wolf nor bear can reach them and where indeed man himself would in many instancies find a similar deficiency; yet these anamal bound from rock to rock and stand apparently in the most careless manner on the sides of precipices of many hundred feet."[48]

While Lewis was occupied with river navigation and descriptive zoology, Clark had other work to do. This day saw a reversal of their usual roles. Clark most often stayed with the main body of the expedition; Lewis often ranged out in company with only a hunter or two. But on May 25 Lewis was on the river while Clark did shore duty. If Lewis had the naturalist's eye, Clark had all the skills of a gifted geographer and cartographer. His frontier childhood and extensive military experience joined with an almost-instinctive understanding of landform to create a remarkably talented explorer. Clark's journal entry for May 25 copies Lewis's description of the bighorn sheep and then offers his own observations on the landscape of east-central Montana. On either side of the river Clark saw a "high, broken, and rockey" country bounded by the Bears Paw and Little Rocky mountains to the north and the Judith Mountains to the south. And in the farther distance, he could barely make out the Highwood Mountains near present-day Great Falls, Montana.[49] Just a day later Clark made a memorable judgement on this part of the West. For the first time the explorers were seeing a landscape that did not quite match what Jefferson expected. "This countrey may with propriety I think be termed the Deserts of America, as I do not Conceive any part can ever be Settled, as it is deficent in water, Timber and Too Steep to be tilled."[50] Travelers today find this part of the Missouri designated a Wild and Scenic River. The expedition was soon to enter the White Cliffs—the "scenic" part. What Clark described is, even today, the "wild" part of the river. This was not the place of Thomas Jefferson's fondest dreams, the place to plant the seeds of republican virtue.

The same day, May 25, that the expedition was struggling with its passage through "the Deserts of America," the president was sharing his thoughts about western exploration with another member of his extended Corps of Discovery. William Dunbar, an accomplished botanist and surveyor, had been one of Jefferson's correspondents since 1800. From his plantation "The Forest" near Natchez, Dunbar sent Jefferson valuable geographic information about the southern end of the Louisiana Purchase. Even more important, Dunbar had led an expedition initiated by Jefferson in 1804 up the Red River, into present-day Arkansas, and back to Natchez.

What initially prompted the letter to Dunbar was a perennial exploration problem—the determination of longtitude without an accurate means of telling time. Chronometers were both rare and prone to mishandling. They were also expensive and had to be wound with an almost religious regularity. Jefferson first summarized his several efforts to find a solution to the problem of longitude measurement and then asked for Dunbar's assistance. But what seemed most important that day were thoughts about strategy for continental exploration. Lewis and Clark were deep in the details; Jefferson aimed at the grand generalizations. "The work we are now doing," he told Dunbar, "is, I trust, done for posterity, in such a way that they need not repeat it." Reflecting on what might be the enduring accomplishments of his enlarged Corps of Discovery, Jefferson concluded the letter with what is perhaps his most compelling description of western exploration. "We shall delineate with correctness the great arteries of this great country: those who come after us will extend the ramifications as they become acquainted with them, and fill up the canvas we begin."[51] On a day that found Lewis painting a word picture of an amazing western animal, Jefferson offered the possibility of greater subjects and larger canvases.

It was an appealing image—the West as an empty canvas with the first American explorers as artists making outlines and others later filling in the details. But both Jefferson and his captains knew that the image was distorted, or at best misleading. Substantial portions of the wider West beyond St. Louis had already been explored, named, and mapped by Spanish, French, Russian, and British travelers. Even more important, native people knew the country intimately and then shared that knowledge with European explorers. The American explorers and their patron readily acknowledged an Indian presence on the land. But to define it as "home" for native people in the sense that Virginia or Kentucky had become home for American planters and farmers was perhaps more than either Jefferson or his captains were ready to concede. The West from Monticello caught Jefferson's fancy because it seemed an empty canvas, a place for Americans to paint a promising future. The notion that the canvas already had Indian pictures on it seemed beside the point. Those native drawings would fade in time and simply be forgotten. What counted was the image of the garden West as a blank space, empty but fertile ground for American farmers.

Talking for Empire
The Days of January 4, 1806

Throughout their two and a half year tour of the West, Lewis and Clark had only one extended time when they were not in the presence of Indians. Those were the weeks when the expedition made its way through present-day Montana, looking for the Shoshones and struggling toward the Continental Divide. Most

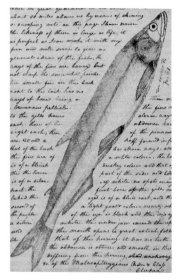

Candle fish from Lewis's journal (American Philosophical Society).

days were like January 4, 1806 at Fort Clatsop on the Oregon coast. Built in December, 1805 along the banks of what is now the Lewis and Clark River, Fort Clatsop was the most distant American outpost in Jefferson's West. It would be the expedition's home until late March 1806. Like so many other Fort Clatsop days, this one was unremarkable in its routine of hunting, cooking, mending, and trading with native neighbors. That Saturday it was wet, cloudy, and, as Lewis glumly noted, the sun was visible for only two hours during the day. It was what the expedition had come to expect from a climate so unlike any they had yet experienced. And as usual, the day with filled with Indians, Indian talk, and talk about Indians. Just the day before, in the midst of a fierce thunderstorm, a group of Clatsops had come from their nearby village, at what is

today Point Adams, to trade and talk. The Clatsops were no strangers to bargaining with Europeans. Ships in the maritime fur trade regularly put in to deal with the Clatsops and their Chinook neighbors. Led by village headman Coboway, the Indians had done a brisk business with the Americans. Trade in foodstuffs—fish and roots—had become an important part of life at Fort Clatsop. And just as the Clatsop people did business with their more distant neighbors, they now found a ready market with the bearded strangers. While the American explorers never found pounded salmon as tasty as roast buffalo, the trade was essential to expedition survival. And the Corps of Discovery welcomed Coboway and his kinsmen, describing them as "mild, inoffensive people."

But there was something that stuck in the craw of the expedition. Lewis and Clark had always fancied themselves masters of the marketplace. As farmers, planters, and hunters the Americans were no strangers to the world of price and profit, contract and commodity. Men from Virginia, Kentucky, and the Illinois country knew all about getting the best prices for horses and land, slaves and tobacco. Or at least they thought they did. That a native people who seemed to Lewis and Clark's eyes ill-clad, squatted on their haunches like frogs, and spoke an unintelligible language could be more tenacious and skillful in bargaining than any sharp American seemed somehow offensive. Perhaps the Clatsop merchants challenged American identity in some fundamental, yet unspoken way. Confronted by Indians who placed deal-making near the center of life and understood trading as both commerce and culture, the captains were quick to label their neighbors as "great higlers in trade." And this was no compliment. Tempted by the fashion of linking particular cultural traits to something vaguely called "national character," Lewis and Clark decided that Clatsop business practices really revealed an "avaricious all grasping disposition." Clatsops were not only greedy but they failed, so the explorers insisted, to understand the relationship between price and value in the marketplace.

All of this prompted the captains to recall one particularly revealing incident—revealing both coastal Indian values and the expedition's misunderstanding of them. Some days before, perhaps in mid-December, a Chinook from across the Columbia came to the post looking to do business. What he had to offer was a small sea otter skin that Lewis dismissed as "small and inferior." Whatever its quality, the American decided to test his notions about Columbia River Indian economic values. "In order to satisfy myself on this subject," Lewis offered his watch, two knives, and a good number of trade beads. That was surely a substantial price to pay for one skin, and the Chinook visitor quickly sensed a bargain in the making. Upping the ante, he demanded twice the number of beads Lewis initially offered. When Lewis refused, the deal fell apart—but only for a day. The next day the Indian was back and the ballet of offer and counter-offer began once again. Eventually Lewis got the sea otter skin and paid with only a few strands of beads. The whole affair persuaded Lewis that his native neighbors were both greedy and foolish. Those same neighbors were perhaps equally convinced that the strangers in the log house did not know the first thing about the real meaning of trade as social ritual as well as economic exchange.[52]

While the Corps of Discovery spent the fourth day of the new year complaining that Indians were either better bargainers or worse capitalists than themselves, the President of the United States was equally involved in Indian affairs. Parties of Indians "coming to treat" with new white neighbors had been part of the American encounter for centuries. The delegations Jefferson ordered Lewis and Clark to organize and send down the Missouri and on to Washington were part of that venerable tradition. On January 4 Jefferson addressed a long and important letter to a group of Missouri River chiefs and headmen—a party that included Osage, Oto, Iowa, Sioux, Missouria, and Arikara representatives. What Jefferson said that day amounted to more than one "treaty talk" for one delegation. The letter was really a proclamation announcing the presence of an American empire and a preview of things to come.

The announcement came first. Quickly dismissing any thought that white Americans were newcomers to the country, Jefferson claimed that "we seem like you to have grown out of this land: we consider ourselves no longer of the old nations beyond the great water, but as united in one family with our red brethern."[53] Talk about the West always fired Jefferson's imagination, and this version of the American past was more fantasy than history. As recent Jefferson biographer Joseph Ellis writes, the West had an "almost mystical place in his thinking."[54] It was an appealing image—two peoples growing out of the same earth and now joined as one family to share the bounty of that earth. But this was an image without consequence, a symbol without substance. There might some day be one family living in this empire of liberty, but no native person or tribe could long doubt that the father and the elders ruled by force from the federal city on the Potomac. The assembled Indians were told that their French, Spanish, and British fathers were gone, never to return. What now spread from Mexico to Canada was an American nation. Jefferson's announcement of imperial domain carried both a threat and a promise. "We are now your fathers," he insisted, "and you shall not lose by the change."

The new Great Father then skillfully used the Lewis and Clark expedition as a bridge between his imperial announcement and a dark promise for the shape of the future. Borrowing a powerful image from Indian diplomacy of the eastern woodlands, Jefferson promised to forge a chain of friendship between the American nation and the peoples of the Missouri. The first link had already been made when the tribes welcomed Lewis and Clark. Acknowledging that welcome, Jefferson promised to follow the explorers' advice about the location of trading posts. The fur trade would be the second link in a growing chain of prosperity, peace, and friendship. This was sweet talk, the kind of paternalistic rhetoric generations of American presidents and politicians would inflict on native people. If the president expected all this to be meekly accepted by the native diplomats, he was headed for a painful surprise.

But in this diplomatic dance Jefferson was still leading. Indians patiently waited their turn, knowing that their steps would be quite different from those of the Great Father. No Indian delegate missed what was behind the announcement and the thank you. Native people had no real choice whether to accept or reject the new American order. Armed force and a burgeoning population made acceptance inevitable. "We are become," so Jefferson bragged, "as numerous as the leaves of the trees, and tho' we do not boast, we do not fear any nation." Native nations should now make peace with all their neighbors. But for all this talk about a peaceable kingdom, the president's words sounded surprisingly threatening. "My children," he reminded his visitors, "we are strong, we are numerous as the stars in the heavens, and we are all gun-men. Yet we live in peace with all nations."[55] Despite words about one family on common ground, the image of an American nation armed and on the move must have made a powerful impression on Indians who ventured east to meet yet another Great Father.

If Jefferson expected the assembled Indians to quickly form a line and eagerly sign up as junior partners in the American business of empire, he was sorely mistaken. While grateful for the opportunity to visit what they called the "Grand lodge of prosperity," the Indians openly admitted that their trip had sparked both fear and dissention. Some friends had counselled against making the journey, "alledging that we would be unwelcome and all of us should die." But now they had survived the trip and were not about to keep silent. Jefferson may have been charmed by his own imaginary American past and future; Indians were not. They simply ignored all the talk about common destiny and went right to what they saw as the most pressing frontier questions.

Two issues led their list of concerns. First, there was the matter of commercial relations between Indians and American traders. Jefferson placed considerable faith in the mutually beneficial consequences of the fur trade and the federal fur trade factory system. That system, first established in 1796, aimed at protecting Indians from unscrupulous white traders. Indian diplomats were much less convinced. "Look sharp," they warned the president, "and tell your men to take not too much fur for a little goods." Native people might not have embraced all the values of market capitalism, but they certainly understood the difference between a bargain and a gouge. Second, and perhaps most important from an Indian perspective, was the behavior of whites on the Missouri River frontier. Indian diplomats agreed that Jefferson's words and intentions appeared honorable. But long experience had taught them that there was a great distance between such noble words from faraway officials and the everyday relations between natives and newcomers. That distance was measured not only in miles but by the countless slights and shoves Indians suffered at the hands of their new neighbors. As the Indian delegation bluntly put it: "You tell us that your children of this side of the Mississippi hear your Word, you are Mistaken, Since every day they Rise their Tomahawks over our heads. You may tell your white children on our lands, to follow your orders, and do not as they please, for they do not keep your word. Our brothers who came here before told us you had ordered good things to be done and sent to our villages, but we have seen nothing, and your waged men [federal Indian agents] think that truth will not reach your ears." But these Indians, far from home and in a strange place, were determined to speak the truth "to the ears of our fathers." In return they expected that government officials would "open their ears to truth to get in." Perhaps they expected too much. Jefferson heard what he chose to hear, imagined as real what he dreamed to be true. That day, as on so many other days, Indian complaints and concerns fell on deaf ears.[56]

Like other representative days on the expedition's calendar, this one offers us many voices talking about Jefferson's West and the Lewis and Clark journey through it. Here are the voices of Indians coming to trade at Fort Clatsop. And here too are the voices of Lewis and Clark at once praising Columbia River peoples as "mild and inoffensive" yet condemning them as sharp and greedy traders. And eastward a continent away the dialogue continued with Jefferson lecturing Indians on the coming American century in the West. Not to be outdone, Indian voices spoke their version of the truth about crafty traders and incompetent agents. In those voices we hear the drama of the West being played out as each set of actors and each script demanded center stage.

This was the kind of day that revealed how American empire in the West might play its final scenes. However defined—whether by geography or diplomacy—the American West would become yet another arena where peoples from many backgrounds would meet each other and then be compelled to deal with the consequences of those meetings. While some of those encounters—including many throughout the course of the expedition—were marked by peace and cooperation, more often the clash of values and habits prompted violence, misunderstanding, or the threat of violence. While never courting trouble, Jefferson's instructions for the Corps of Discovery implied that violence was not only possible but probable. And as Jefferson's voice made plain that day, a western country now part of the United States would be American by the power of guns and a restless, westering population. Finally, and of no small importance, Indian voices within Jefferson's own hearing spoke for compromise, justice, and mutual understanding. As they put it that day, "we wish to live like you and be men like you."[57] These men and their kinfolk at home had no intention of becoming white Americans. What they sought was some middle place, some shared space for both peoples to live ordinary lives in that extraordinary place called the American West.

Sage grouse from Clark's journal (Missouri Historical Society).

COUNTRIES OF THE MIND

In early October 1805, while the Corps of Discovery was resting with the Nez Perce Indians after the harrowing crossing of the Lolo Trail, Thomas Jefferson was busy sorting out the natural history specimens Lewis had sent from Fort Mandan. As he told Charles Willson Peale, some of those items were bound for an "Indian hall" at Monticello.[58] Seeds collected by the explorers went to the plantation garden. In the years that followed visitors to Jefferson's house on the little mountain often commented on those remarkable things and what they might mean. When the French aristocrat Baron de Montlezun visited Monticello in 1816 he saw not only the mounted head of a bighorn but several buffalo hide drawings and maps done by Indians. One drawing, illustrating a battle, was particularly striking with its lines of warriors mounted on horses painted bright red and green.[59]

Visitors to Monticello today see only two authentic Lewis and Clark artifacts—a set of elk antlers and a silhouette of Lewis. All the rest of the wonderful things the expedition provided to Jefferson's Indian hall were scattered and much was lost. Those bits and pieces of the Lewis and Clark journey were at Monticello not only for interior decoration but as reminders of the expedition and its accomplishments. While Jefferson claimed that the "Lewis and Clark tour" had "all the success which could have been expected," perhaps the things gathered on this voyage of discovery also remained him that the great trek to the Pacific was not all he hoped it would be.[60] And those hopes had been very great. They ranged from grand plans for securing the future of the republic in the West to discoveries of plants and animals new to European science. Lewis and Clark were scouting countries of the mind as well as territories for an expanding nation.

For all those high hopes, or perhaps because of them, expedition realities did not quite measure up to Jefferson's vision. The distance between the West as imagined in the instructions for Lewis and the country as found by the explorers came clear as soon as Jefferson read the first letter Lewis sent on returning to St.

Elk antlers acquired by Lewis and Clark on display in the Monticello Entrance Hall (University of Virginia Department of Biology).

Louis in September 1806. Placed side by side, Jefferson's letter of instructions in 1803 and the report from Lewis represent expedition bookends—a confident beginning and an ambiguous conclusion.

Lewis knew what the president meant when he talked about the "object of your mission." Whatever else the Corps of Discovery might have accomplished, whether in science or diplomacy, it was the passage through the West and an evaluation of the republican garden that really mattered. Now at the end of the expedition's formal journey, Lewis and Clark knew that Jefferson's optimistic geography did not match western realities. The view from Monticello did not fit what the captains saw from Lemhi Pass. When Lewis and Clark stood at the Continental Divide in August 1805, they saw snow-clad mountains, range upon range to the horizon. There was no direct water communication across the continent by way of the Missouri and the Columbia. Moving the fabled northwest passage south from the arctic to what is today Montana and Idaho proved a grand illusion and an equally grand deception. And the West as garden? Jefferson imagined the West as a single, fertile region. Lewis and Clark now knew by experience the West as a place of great variety in climate and landform. If parts of the Missouri River valley could be a farmers' paradise, other sections of the West were "deserts" sure to defeat even the most virtuous republican. But how to tell the president that his geographic foundation for the future of the republic was built on suspect terrain?

Lewis's September 23 letter is a masterpiece of ambiguity, an exercise in sleight-of-hand. On one hand, Lewis confidently assured the president that the expedition "had discovered the most practicable rout which dose exist across the Continent." But what he gave with one hand the explorer snatched away with the other. The route was not a genuine water passage and it was surely not practical for the sorts of bulky agricultural products that Jefferson had in mind. Western rivers were quite unlike those that flowed to the Atlantic. Lewis grudgingly admitted that the land passage, while perhaps useful for the expansion of the American fur trade, was hardly a broad highway to and through the West. The expedition had not found Jefferson's simple western geography. Lewis reluctantly admitted that the northern overland route charted by the Corps of Discovery could never take the place of sea lanes around the Cape of Good Hope. As he delicately put it, the overland passage blazed by the expedition was useful only for good "not bulky brittle nor of a verry perishable nature."[61] If Jefferson had any hopes for a water transportation system linking western farms to global markets, Lewis put an end to it. Some parts of the West might be the fertile garden of Jefferson's imagination, but profit-minded farmers would plow no ground without promise of profit. In one sense the expedition had failed in the very way that Attorney-General Levi Lincoln feared. There was no "communication" through the garden. What poet Walt Whitman called "the passage to India" would not come until the days of the Oregon Trail and the transcontinental railroad. And because there was no passage, perhaps the future of the republic and the promise of renewal in the West now seemed less certain. What we see some two centuries later as a momentous event in the history of the American West must have appeared less triumphant in late October 1806 as Jefferson studied that slippery letter from Lewis.

Thomas Jefferson and the Corps of Discovery made parallel journeys through the West. Lewis and Clark moved through visible landscapes; Jefferson's journey had always been in the country of the imagination. And that odyssey was by no means finished when his captains reached St. Louis. Jefferson now began a different kind of voyage, a search for the Corps of Discovery's place in the historical scheme of things. Just as he had created the expedition, now Jefferson sought to shape both present and future understandings of the enterprise. If the search for the passage failed to disclose that ever-elusive piece of geography, there were sure to be other reasons for celebration. By the time Lewis reached Washington in late December 1806, Jefferson must have begun to realize that the captains and their commander had just started an uncertain march into the country of meanings, reputations, and legacies.

Jefferson's first steps in that journey directly involved Lewis. Essential to any reshaping of the expedition and its work was the publication of Lewis's expedition report. Jefferson had read and admired published accounts drawn from the travels of Sir Alexander Mackenzie, Captain James Cook, and Captain George Vancouver. Those explorers, and often their ghostwriters, took unedited travel journals and transformed them into connected narratives. Such books usually had

California condor from Lewis's journal (American Philosophical Society).

a well-defined cast of characters and a plot line that followed the journey from beginning to end. Jefferson was intent on having Lewis write such a literary account, one that could be appreciated by all sorts of readers. Like his colleagues at the American Philosophical Society, Jefferson believed that useful knowledge demanded a wide audience. Knowledge not shared by means of print and publication was knowledge wasted and lost. Whatever Lewis and Clark learned needed to be spread abroad. With that in mind, Jefferson began a not-so-subtle campaign to shape Lewis the traveler into Lewis the author. Each letter, and certainly each private conversation, contained some hint or nudge toward writing the narrative. That effort, ultimately unsuccessful, lasted until Lewis's death in 1809. At the same time, and because Lewis's volumes seemed painfully slow in coming, Jefferson found himself responding to individual requests for expedition materials from scholars like Benjamin Smith Barton, Charles Willson Peale, and Bernard McMahon.

It was in that correspondence with members of what Jefferson liked to call "the republic of science" that he most fully re-imagined the expedition and its meaning. Whether he recognized it or not, this part of Jefferson's journey into the country of fame and reputation was guided by what Levi Lincoln suggested some years before. In a prophetic moment, Lincoln proposed that if the travelers did not find the passage or were forced to return short of the Pacific, reputation could be rescued by claiming discoveries in the world of knowledge. And claiming such discoveries would put the American exploration enterprise on the high moral ground as well. Others had come for conquest; Americans could assert more noble motives. By the summer of 1808 Jefferson had faced the failure of his passage vision and now busied himself offering a view of the expedition much like the one Lincoln presented. Writing to French naturalist Bernard Lacépède, Jefferson now asserted that "the addition to our knolege, in every department, resulting from that tour, of Messrs. Lewis and Clark, has entirely fulfilled my expectation."[62] Levi Lincoln had been right. Science—in the shape of exotic animals, strange Indians, and useful plants—might save the whole venture from embarrassment and oblivion.

The emphasis on scientific accomplishment also fit Lewis's own changing conception of the expedition. When Lewis wrote Clark in June 1803 inviting him to join the expedition, he placed greatest emphasis on the search for the passage to the Pacific. Only at the end of the letter did Lewis mention that "the objects of this mission are scientific."[63] Four years later science headed the expedition's accomplishment list. In the spring of 1807 Philadelphia printer John Conrad issued a prospectus for Lewis's proposed exploration narrative. The narrative would come in three volumes, with handsome illustrations and useful maps. This would surely be a fitting monument for the expedition and its place in the larger history of enlightenment exploration. Lewis intended that the first volume be "a narrative of the voyage, with a description of some of the most remarkable places in those hitherto unknown wilds of America." Here was

Vine maple leaf from Lewis's journal (American Philosophical Society).

the tale of adventure eagerly sought by a wider audience. But in keeping with the new emphasis on science, Lewis promised two full volumes packed with botany, ethnography, zoology, and "other natural phenomena."[64] In many ways Lewis's prospectus and Jefferson's letters were a formal announcement of the new wisdom about the expedition. Any thoughts about the passage seemed lost in the light of glowing promises of memorable scientific advances. The western garden would surely someday see farmers working the land. For the moment, the gardeners were going to be men of science and commerce.

And the reading public seemed ready to embrace this view of the expedition. Michel Amoureux, a French exile living in New Madrid, Louisiana Territory, wrote asking Lewis to put his name on the subscription list. New York artist John

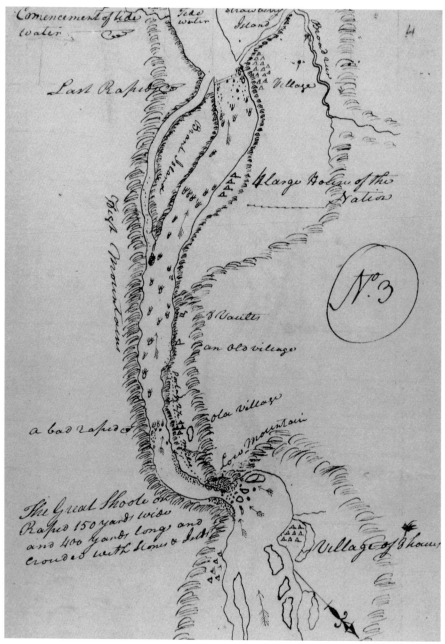

Map entitled "Great Rapids of the Columbia" from Clark's journal (American Philosophical Society).

T. Jones offered his professional services for engraving maps and plates. Luther Robbins and three of his Maine neighbors had their names added to the buyers list. And Baptist preacher William Woods went so far as to send Lewis $31.00 in advance of publication.[65] For all of Jefferson's letters to friends and his prodding of Lewis, the success of the re-shaped expedition depended on the explorer-turned-author and timely publication. To his credit, Lewis did make preliminary plans for printing the work. Arrangements were also in place for engraving plates and maps. The only thing lacking was a completed manuscript. Despite regular reminders and even some scolding from Jefferson, Lewis could not seem to write a single line. Adrift in a sea of troubles both personal and political, Lewis found neither voice nor pen to fashion what Jefferson now wanted most of all. At the time of Lewis's death in 1809, the publishers wrote Jefferson with the sorry news that "Govr. Lewis never furnished us with a line of the M.S. nor indeed could we ever hear any thing from him respecting it tho frequent applications to that effect were made to him."[66]

Lewis's failure as an author and his sad death initiated a complex set of events that finally led William Clark to engage the services of Philadelphia lawyer and writer Nicholas Biddle. Biddle finally brought to press in 1814—almost a decade after the expedition—essentially what Lewis proposed as his first volume. Here, in a meager printing of only 1,417 copies, was the expedition story as a western adventure. Readers would find an engaging tale of travel across the continent, but no science. The Corps of Discovery had been denied the passage by the unforgiving realities of geography. Now that company of travelers had its place in the empire of the mind taken away as well. As Jefferson lamented to distinguished naturalist and geographer Alexander Von Humboldt, "the botanical and zoological discoveries of Lewis will probably experience greater delay, and become known to the world thro other channels."[67] And as fate would have it, those "other channels" proved as elusive as any northwest passage. At the time of the nation's centennial in 1876, Lewis and Clark had almost vanished from the landscape of American memory. Now the western heroes were explorers like John Charles Frémont or colorful figures from the pages of dime novels.

FILLING UP THE CANVAS

Looking west from Monticello in 1803 Thomas Jefferson imagined a small exploring party making a simple "tour" into a promising place. One officer and ten or twelve men could make the journey to the Pacific and back with time to spare. And the West itself seemed the chosen place to guarantee the future of the republic against the forces of political tyranny and social decay. A decade later, with the nation deep in the War of 1812 and the expedition's account still unpublished, neither the journey nor the West appreared all that simple or promising. There was no easy portage over the mountains from Atlantic to Pacific waters. Nor was the West quite the wonderland of volcanoes, strange animals, and Welsh Indians some hoped to find. But for all these confusions and disappointments, the Lewis and Clark journey through Jefferson's West did make an enduring difference—a difference that Jefferson may not have fully appreciated, but one that is clearer two centuries later.

The emblematic days recounted here all point to a uniquely American vision for the future of the West. The Lewis and Clark expedition exemplified that vision and first carried it beyond the wide Missouri. Some two centuries after the Lewis and Clark journey, the shape of that vision and some of its implications and consequences are now in sharper focus.

Jefferson never doubted that in one way or another the West was bound to be American in language and political culture. And most likely that American West was going to be divided up into new states belonging to the federal union. In one of his most memorable expressions of America's continental future, Jefferson wrote: "Our confederacy must be viewed as the next from which all America, North and South, is to be peopled." It was only a matter of time until Spain's vast North American empire would slip into the hands of the United States. "My fear," Jefferson told Archibald Stuart in 1786, "is that they are too feeble to hold them until our population can be sufficiently advanced to gain it from them piece by piece."[68] The sheer force of an expanding population made an American empire in the West a foregone conclusion—or so it seemed.

By 1803, in light of the Louisiana Purchase, Jefferson seemed even more confident about the future of the West as part of the United States. Writing a carefully-worded letter to Senator John C. Breckinridge, Jefferson gave fullest expression to his cultural and political vision for the American West. Federalist critics of territorial expansion in general and the Louisiana Purchase in particular insisted that the newly-acquired lands west of the Mississippi would form a rival nation, one that could endanger the security of the United States. What if, argued the Federalists, the fledglings from the eastern nest fly west and become our commercial rivals or even our military enemies? Jefferson dismissed this as idle fantasy, insisting that "the future inhabitants of the Atlantic and Missipi States will be our sons." Leaving behind the nest image, he offered a new and striking one— one that gave special place to explorers as the vanguard of single expanding republic. "When we shall be full on this side, we may lay off a range of States on the Western bank from the head to the mouth [of the Mississippi], and so, range after range, advancing compactly as we multiply."[69] And that is exactly what modern-day travelers see through the airplane window. This was the imperial vision Lewis and Clark carried when they surveyed the land and told native people about a new Great Father. Writing to William Clark in June 1803, Lewis captured that sense of American empire when he envisioned the explorers proclaiming "the rising importance of the U. States."[70]

A vision of the West as home to an expanded American empire was hardly unique to Jefferson. Geographers like Gilbert Imlay and Jedediah Morse had long predicted that the lands beyond the Mississippi would become part of the American nation. In his *American Geography* (1789), Morse confidently asserted that "We cannot but anticipate the period, as not far distant, when the AMERICAN EMPIRE will comprehend millions of souls, west of the Mississippi."[71] But Jefferson's vision of an American West looked toward a somewhat different future. The West would not only be part of the American nation but it would be the foundation for what he confidently called the "empire for liberty." Writing to James Madison three years after the return of the Corps of Discovery, Jefferson predicted that "we should have such an empire for liberty as she has never surveyed since the creation: and I am persuaded no constitution was ever before so well calculated as ours for extensive empire and self-government."[72] Linking together two such dissimilar words—"empire" and "liberty"—was Jefferson at his imaginative and audacious best. The American empire in the West could renew the republic, preserve its ideological integrity, and allow citizens of the nation to avoid charges of empire-building for base motives. The Spanish, French, and British empires were all founded on and perpetuated monarchy and tyranny. Jefferson's explorers were engaged in marking out an empire for liberty.

Jefferson and those who shared his passion for the United States encompassing the continent were persuaded that the American West would turn a profit. While always wary of the excesses of luxury, he never doubted that profit was a worthy reason for making homes on the range. Commerce of all sorts would define the American West in the way that missionary zeal had marked the Spanish empire. In late November 1806, after reading a detailed report on Pacific Northwest trade drafted by Meriwether Lewis, Jefferson expressed the hope that "some enterprizing mercantile Americans" would head to the Columbia River and settle there.[73] At that moment no one was more enterprising than New York fur merchant John Jacob Astor. In 1811 his Pacific Fur Company established Fort Astoria at the mouth of the Columbia, the first American commercial outpost in the far West. And in the century to come the West would be flooded with many more enterprising and mercantile Americans. In large part they came because explorers like Lewis and Clark reported that the West promised profit and a fresh start.

The Jeffersonian vision that Lewis and Clark carried saw the West as a place of settlement, a farmers' paradise. Perhaps it was William Clark who understood that best. He and his family were part of a settling and planting tradition, one that came from Virginia to Kentucky and then on to the Missouri country. As superintendent for Indian affairs in the West—a post he assumed in 1807—he always talked about the West as an agricultural homeland for white settlers as well as Indians dispossessed by the federal removal policy. The Lewis and Clark expedition stands near the beginning of the American version of the West as the garden of the world. Gardens in the West had been a feature of exploration thinking and writing since the Age of Columbus. But it was Jefferson and Gallatin who put explorers into the West not so much as fur-trade pathfinders but as agricultural extension agents. There would be other visions of the western landscape, including notions of the Great American Desert as advanced by Zebulon Montgomery Pike and Stephen H. Long. But the Jeffersonian garden, rooted in the Lewis and Clark expedition, never lost its appeal for all sorts of Americans. Real estate speculators, irrigation engineers, federal policy planners, and generations of ordinary farmers—all saw the West as Jefferson's garden. The journeys they made to places like Kansas, Nebraska, and the Dakotas, and Oregon were always made in the footsteps of Lewis and Clark. What overland travelers followed was not the Lewis and Clark trail but the vision of the West conjured up by Jefferson and then advanced by the Corps of Discovery.

An important Shoshone oral tradition still alive long after Cameahwait's people met the Corps of Discovery described the Americans as "men with faces pale as ashes."[74] What did the presence of those ash faces mean for the future of native people in the West? Jefferson promised that Indians who acknowledged the new Great Father would not "lose by the change." And important tribal leaders like Cameahwait, Twisted Hair, and Yelleppit welcomed the expedition as the sign of a prosperous, secure future. Day after day, for nearly two and a half years, the Corps of Discovery lived in relative peace and harmony with its native neighbors. William Clark captured that sense of a peaceful journey when he told Indians: "We have been to the great lake of the west and are now on our return to my country. I have seen all my red children quite to that great lake and talked with them, and taken them by the hand of their great father the Great Chief of all the white people."[75] All the paternalism in those words should not blind us to the fact that on most days native people and the Corps of Discovery shared a common life in the West.

Yet there were days in the life of the expedition marked by deceit and violence. There were moments when the present was dark and the future cloudy, when loss plainly overwhelmed gain. When Lewis and Clark needed an extra canoe for the homeward journey from Fort Clatsop, they stole one from the Clatsop village, and betrayed Coboway's trust. And in an explosion of fury and violence, Lewis and a small party killed two Piegan Blackfeet when the Indians attempted to take expedition guns and horses. The deaths of two Indians at the Two Medicine River in present-day north-central Montana in late July 1806 was more than just a frontier skirmish. In a bold act of imperial bravado, Lewis ripped the sacred amulets from the warriors' shields and then hung a peace medal around the neck of Side Hill Calf, one of the dead Piegans. He did that, as he later explained to Clark, so other Indians would "be informed who we were."[76] If this was an empire for liberty, it was also an empire that could strike back with force and vengeance. Jefferson might promise the kind hand of a Great Father; Lewis's hand held out another sort of future.

Finally and perhaps most important, Jefferson knew that the Lewis and Clark journey was about knowledge and the process of knowing. Before the expedition made its western tour, speculation and conjecture dominated any discussions about the lands beyond St. Louis. The West might be home to packs of llamas or herds of mammoths. There might be vast inland seas or miles of salt mountains. Indians might be dwarves or giants or even the children of lost tribes from Wales or Israel. And most compelling, the West might be an endless Eden, a place to outrun the troubled past and find a promising tomorrow. Those kinds of dreams and illusions would not vanish after 1806. There would be generations of hopeful, sometimes deluded men and women bent on spinning fantasies in the West. Jefferson's geography of hope and renewal would not lose its appeal for a long time, if ever. But the experience of the Lewis and Clark expedition marked a beginning in the slow process of replacing fiction with fact, speculation with information. What had been in shadow and dream was now present in substance and reality.

Nothing illustrates this more graphically than comparing maps of Louisiana available to the expedition in 1804 and the William Clark map published in 1814 to accompany the Biddle narrative. In 1804 the cartographer Samuel Lewis prepared a map of Louisiana as part of Aaron Arrowsmith's New and Elegant Atlas of North America. That map expressed in unmistakable terms Jefferson's hopeful geography. Samuel Lewis's portrayal of the West promised explorers the sort of river system Jefferson was sure might take them to the Pacific.

And if the map was to be believed, mountains would be no barrier for such a journey. The Rockies were but one thin range of mountains, and the Cascades simply did not exist. When Lewis and Clark saw a map prepared by St. Louis cartographer Antoine Soulard, what had been geographic faith appeared to become scientific reality. Soulard prepared his map of the West from the most reliable information available in St. Louis. His picture of the West offered the same terrain features present in Samuel Lewis's map. This was the simple West, a place where geography seemed allied to empire for the benefit of the American republic.

A decade later, thanks to the Corps of Discovery and a whole generation of geographically-minded fur traders, the American map of the West looked dramatically different. In December 1810 Clark sent Nicholas Biddle his master map of the West. Based on explorer and trapper experience but still carrying some old dreams, that map was given special authority when engraved as "Map of Lewis and Clark's Track Across the Western Portion of North America." What had been all simplicity in 1804 was now replaced by complexity. Western rivers and mountains took remarkably accurate shape. And gone was the hope that the Missouri and the Columbia would form a northwest passage for westering Americans. But dreams die hard, and even in Clark's map there remained a hint of another passage. Clark fashioned a new north-south water highway, this one based on a ghost river named the Multnomah. During their exploration of the Columbia, Lewis and Clark heard about a river known today as the Willamette. Drawing on Indian information garbled in translation, the captains conjured up the Multnomah—a river that would haunt explorers for the next thirty years. Clark sketched the Multnomah from its junction with the Columbia to its headwaters in a region he believed also gave rise to the Yellowstone, Platte, Bighorn, Arkansas, Colorado, and Rio Grande. If travelers could trace the Multnomah to its source, it might be possible to cross over to other western rivers that drained into the Missouri. Perhaps a passage might yet be found. The history of geographic exploration never moves in a straight line, marching directly from old illusions to new realities. Knowledge of whatever sort comes clear by shades and degrees. At the same time, Clark's map remains a powerful statement of the expedition's contribution

Samuel Lewis's "Map of Louisiana, 1804" (Gilcrease Museum).

"Map of Lewis and Clark's Track" copied by Samuel Lewis from original drawing by William Clark printed in 1814 (Library of Congress).

to the expansion of reliable geographic knowledge. In the eyes of mapmakers the West would never look the same.

In a memorable letter to William Dunbar written while the Corps of Discovery was still in the West, Jefferson described his vision for future western exploration in nearly lyrical terms. A whole company of travelers would "fill up the canvas we begin."[77] William Clark's map was the outline for an American West— the West Jefferson first invented in his spacious imagination and then sent Lewis and Clark to find and explore. What remained was to sketch in the details. There would surely be more ventures West, more memorable days. The Lewis and Clark journey marked a whole range of beginnings and endings, openings and closings. The distinctly American West begins with Jefferson and the Corps of Discovery. Guided and informed by Jefferson's instructions, Lewis and Clark saw the West in terms of national power, personal profit, and unlimited opportunity. In their maps and in their minds, by what they did and what they wrote, Lewis and Clark imprinted Jefferson's western vision on a westering nation. The country between the Missouri and the Pacific, and the people who called it home, would never be the same. By whatever calculation, whether for gain or loss, Lewis and Clark edged the West toward an American future.

Suggested Reading

The literature of the Lewis and Clark expedition is both vast in size and varied in quality. Much the same can be said for writing about Thomas Jefferson. Any reader making a voyage of discovery into Jefferson, the West, and the Corps of Discovery must begin with Donald Jackson, *Thomas Jefferson and the Stony Mountains: Exploring the West from Monticello* (Urbana: University of Illinois Press, 1981; reprint, Norman: University of Oklahoma Press, 1993). Also useful at the beginning of the journey is Stephen E. Ambrose, *Undaunted Courage: Meriwether Lewis, Thomas Jefferson, and the Opening of the American West* (New York: Simon and Schuster, 1996). For those seeking to follow in the footsteps of Lewis and Clark there are no better guides than Roy E. Appleman, *Lewis and Clark: Historic Places Associated with Their Transcontinental Exploration (1804-06)* (Washington, D.C: Government Printing Office, 1975; reprint, St. Louis: Jefferson National Expansion Historical Association, 1993) and Dayton Duncan, *Out West: An American Journey* (New York: Viking, 1987).

Donald Jackson once called Lewis and Clark "the writingest explorers" in American history. Nothing can take the place of reading the words written by members of the Corps of Discovery. The definitive edition of the Lewis and Clark journal is Gary E. Moulton, ed., *The Journals of the Lewis and Clark Expedition*, 13 vols. (Lincoln: University of Nebraska Press, 1983-1999). The best one-volume edition of the journals is Frank Bergon, ed., *The Journals of Lewis and Clark* (New York: Penguin Books, 1989). Readers of the journals will soon find Donald Jackson, ed., *Letters of the Lewis and Clark Expedition with Related Documents, 1783-1854*, 2 vols. Second Edition, (Urbana: University of Illinois Press, 1978) to be of great value.

Thanks to the efforts of Donald Jackson in renewing Lewis and Clark scholarship, there are now many fine books on various aspects of the Lewis and Clark expedition. Among the most useful are: John L. Allen, *Passage through the Garden: Lewis and Clark and the Image of the American Northwest* (Urbana:

University of Illinois Press, 1975; reprinted as *Lewis and Clark and the Image of the American Northwest* (Mineola, New York: Dover Publications, 1991), Daniel B. Botkin, *Our Natural History: The Lessons of Lewis and Clark* (New York: G. P. Putnam's Sons, 1995; reprint, New York: Berkley Publishing Group, 1996), Paul R. Cutright, *Lewis and Clark: Pioneering Naturalists* (Urbana: University of Illinois Press, 1969; reprint, Lincoln: University of Nebraska Press, 1989), Albert Furtwangler, *Acts of Discovery: Visions of America in the Lewis and Clark Journals* (Urbana: University of Illinois Press, 1993), and James P. Ronda, *Lewis and Clark among the Indians* (Lincoln: University of Nebraska Press, 1984). James P. Ronda's *Voyages of Discovery: Essays on the Lewis and Clark Expedition* (Helena: Montana Historical Society Press, 1998) provides a convenient collection of important essays and documents relating to the journey and its consequences.

The Lewis and Clark expedition is best understood in the larger context of the exploration of North America. No books do that with more grace and clarity than Bernard DeVoto, *The Course of Empire* (Boston: Houghton, Mifflin, 1952) and William H. Goetzmann, *Exploration and Empire: The Explorer and the Scientist in the Winning of the American West* (New York: Random House, 1966; reprint, Austin: Texas State Historical Association, 1994).

NOTES

1 Clark to Lewis, Clarksville, July 18, 1803, Donald Jackson, ed., *The Letters of the Lewis and Clark Expedition with Related Documents, 1783-1854.* Revised Edn., 2 vols. (Urbana: University of Illinois Press, 1978), 1:111. Hereafter cited as *Letters.*

2 Lewis to Jefferson, Fort Mandan, April 7, 1805, *Letters,* 1:231-236.

3 Jefferson to John Barnes, Monticello, August 12, 1805, Jefferson Papers, Microfilm edition, Library of Congress, Washington, D.C.

4 Jefferson to Madison, Monticello, August 17, 1805, James Morton Smith, ed., *The Republic of Letters: The Correspondence between Thomas Jefferson and James Madison, 1776-1826,* 3 vols. (New York: W.W. Norton, 1995), 3:1379.

5 Jefferson to Etienne Lemaire, Monticello, August 17, 1805, *Letters,* 1:255. Lemaire's letter to Jefferson is in *Letters,* 1: 253-54.

6 The expedition's activities for August 17, 1805 are detailed in Gary E. Moulton, ed., *The Journals of the Lewis and Clark Expedition,* 13 vols. (Lincoln: University of Nebraska Press, 1983-1999), 5: 109-116. Hereafter cited as *JLCE.* Lewis's comments on the night of August 16-17 are at 5: 106.

7 Jefferson to Charles Bellini, Paris, September 30, 1785, Julian Boyd, et al., eds., *The Papers of Thomas Jefferson,* 27 vols. to date (Princeton: Princeton University Press, 1950—), 8: 568.

8 Jefferson to Adams, Monticello, June 11, 1812, Lester J. Cappon, ed., *The Adams-Jefferson Correspondence,* 2 vols. (Chapel Hill: University of North Carolina Press, 1959), 2: 307.

9 Juan Gassiot to Felipe de Neve Arizpe, Sonora, October 9, 1783, quoted in David J. Weber, *The Spanish Frontier in North America* (New Haven: Yale University Press, 1992), 271.

10 Donald Jackson, *Thomas Jefferson and the Stony Mountains: Exploring the West from Monticello* (Urbana: University of Illinois Press, 1981), ix.

11 Jefferson to George Rogers Clark, Annapolis, December 4, 1783, *Letters,* 2: 654-55.

12 George Rogers Clark to Jefferson, Richmond, February 8, 1784, *Letters,* 2: 655-56.

13 Jackson, *Thomas Jefferson and the Stony Mountains,* 48-56.

[14] Jefferson to the Rev. James Madison, Paris, July 19, 1788, Boyd, et al., eds., *Jefferson Papers*, 13: 382.

[15] William Peden, ed., *Notes on the State of Virginia* (Chapel Hill: University of North Carolina Press, 1955), 8-9.

[16] Jackson, *Thomas Jefferson and the Stony Mountains*, 74-80.

[17] Jefferson to André Michaux, April 30, 1793, *Letters*, 2: 669-672.

[18] W. Kaye Lamb, ed., *The Journals and Letters of Sir Alexander Mackenzie* (Cambridge, England: Hakluyt Society, 1970), 417.

[19] Jefferson to William Ludlow, Monticello, September 6, 1824, Merrill D. Peterson, ed., *Thomas Jefferson: Writings* (New York: The Library of America, 1984), 1496.

[20] Jefferson to John Jay, Paris, August 23, 1785, Peterson, ed., *Thomas Jefferson: Writings*, 818.

[21] Jefferson to Madison, Paris, December 20, 1787, Smith, ed., *Republic of Letters*, 1: 514.

[22] Jefferson to G. K. van Hogendorp, Paris, October 13, 1785, Boyd, et al., eds., *Jefferson Papers*, 8: 633.

[23] The complex diplomacy of this period is ably discussed in Alexander DeConde, *This Affair of Louisiana* (New York: Charles Scribners Sons, 1976) and Reginald Horsman, *The Diplomacy of the New Republic, 1776-1815* (Arlington Heights, Illinois: Harlan Davidson, 1985).

[24] Carlos Martínez de Yrujo to Pedro Cevallos, December 2, 1802, *Letters*, 1: 4-6.

[25] Peden, ed., *Notes on the State of Virginia*, 5-16.

[26] Jefferson to Lewis, Washington, July 15, 1803, *Letters*, 1: 109 quoting Bernard Lacépède to Jefferson, May 13, 1803, *Letters*, 1: 46-47.

[27] Barry Lopez, *Arctic Dreams: Imagination and Desire in a Northern Landscape* (New York: Charles Scribners Sons, 1986), 256.

[28] John L. Allen, *Passage through the Garden: Lewis and Clark and the Image of the American Northwest* (Urbana: University of Illinois Press, 1975), xix-xxvi.

[29] Joseph J. Ellis, *American Sphinx: The Character of Thomas Jefferson* (New York: Alfred A. Knopf, 1997), 193.

[30] *Letters*, Foreword, v.

[31] James Madison, Notes, April 14, 1803, *Letters*, 1: 34.

[32] Gallatin to Jefferson, Washington, April 13, 1803, *Letters*, 1: 32-34.

[33] Lincoln to Jefferson, Washington, April 17, 1803, *Letters,* 1: 34-36.

[34] Jefferson to Lewis, Washington, June 20, 1803, *Letters,* 1: 61.

[35] Jefferson to Lewis, Washingon, November 16, 1803, *Letters,* 1: 137.

[36] Jefferson to C.F.C. Volney, Washington, February 11, 1806, Peterson, ed., *Jefferson: Writings,* 1159-60.

[37] Jefferson to Lewis, Washington, June 20, 1803, *Letters,* 1: 62-63.

[38] Lewis to Jefferson, Cincinnati, September 28, 1803, *Letters,* 1: 124

[39] *JLCE,* 2: 87-89.

[40] Lewis to Jefferson, Cincinnati, October 3, 1803, *Letters,* 1: 131.

[41] Jefferson to Lewis, Washington, November 16, 1803, *Letters,* 1: 136-39.

[42] *JLCE,* 3: 230.

[43] *JLCE,* 3: 230-31.

[44] Jefferson to Reuben Lewis, Washington, November 6, 1804, *Letters,* 1: 216.

[45] William Least Heat-Moon, *Blue Highways: A Journey into America* (Boston: Little, Brown and Co., 1982), 136.

[46] Charles Gratiot to Lewis, St. Louis, November 13, 1804, *Letters,* 1: 217.

[47] *JLCE,* 10: 92.

[48] *JLCE,* 4: 194-95.

[49] *JLCE,* 4: 198.

[50] *JLCE,* 4: 205-6.

[51] Jefferson to William Dunbar, Washington, May 25, 1805, *Letters,* 1: 245.

[52] *JLCE,,* 6: 165.

[53] Jefferson to the Indian Delegation, Washington, January 4, 1806, *Letters,* 1: 281.

[54] Ellis, *American Sphinx,* 212.

[55] Jefferson to the Indian Delegation, Washington, January 4, 1806, *Letters,* 1: 282.

[56] Indian Speech to Jefferson and the Secretary of War, Washington, January 4, 1806, *Letters,* 1: 284-89.

[57] Ibid., 1: 286.

[58] Jefferson to Charles Willson Peale, Washington, October 6, 1805, *Letters*, 1: 260.

[59] Excerpt from Baron de Montlezun's Journal, September 20, 1806, *Letters*, 2: 733.

[60] Jefferson, Annual Message to Congress, December 2, 1806, *Letters*, 1: 352.

[61] Lewis to Jefferson, St. Louis, September 23, 1806, *Letters*, 1: 321.

[62] Jefferson to Bernard Lacépède, Washington, July 4, 1808, *Letters*, 2: 443.

[63] Lewis to Clark, Washington, June 19, 1803, *Letters*, 1: 59.

[64] Conrad Prospectus, ca. April 1, 1807, *Letters*, 2: 394-6.

[65] Michel Amoureux to Lewis, New Madrid, Louisiana Territory, May 31, 1807, *Letters*, 2: 412-3; John T. Jones to Lewis and Clark, New York, June 13, 1807, *Letters*, 2: 415-6; Luther Robbins to Lewis and Clark, Green, District of Maine, October 11, 1807, *Letters*, 2: 431-2.

[66] C. and A. Conrad and Co. to Jefferson, Philadelphia, November 13, 1809, *Letters*, 2: 469.

[67] Jefferson to Alexander von Humboldt, Monticello, December 6, 1813, *Letters*, 2: 596.

[68] Jefferson to Archibald Stuart, Paris, January 25, 1786, Boyd, et al., eds., *Jefferson Papers*, 9: 218.

[69] Jefferson to John C. Breckinridge, Monticello, August 12, 1803, Peterson, ed., *Jefferson: Writings*, 1138.

[70] Lewis to Clark, Washington, June 19, 1803, *Letters*, 1: 59.

[71] Jedediah Morse, *The American Geography* (Elizabeth Town, New Jersey: Shepard Kollock, 1789), unpaginated Introduction.

[72] Jefferson to Madison, Monticello, April 27, 1809, Smith, ed., *Republic of Letters*, 3: 1586.

[73] Everett S. Brown, ed., *William Plumer's Memorandum of Proceedings in the United States Senate, 1803-1807* (New York: Macmillan Co., 1923), 520.

[74] Thomas J. Farnham, "Travels in the Great Western Prairies" (1843), in R. G. Thwaites, ed., *Early Western Travels*, 28 vols. (Cleveland: Arthur H. Clark Co., 1904-6), 28: 272-3.

[75] *JLCE*, 8: 213.

[76] *JLCE*, 8: 135.

[77] Jefferson to Dunbar, Washington, May 25, 1805, *Letters*, 1: 245.